SURVIVAL Lessons

RESOURCE MATERIAL FOR TEACHERS

DIANE HALL and MARK FOLEY

Nelson

Thomas Nelson and Sons Ltd
Nelson House   Mayfield Road
Walton-on-Thames   Surrey
KT12 5PL UK

51 York Place
Edinburgh
EH1 3JD UK

Thomas Nelson (Hong Kong) Ltd
Toppan Building 10/F
22A Westlands Road
Quarry Bay Hong Kong

Nelson Canada
1120 Birchmount Road
Scarborough Ontario
M1K 5G4 Canada

© Diane Hall and Mark Foley 1990
First published by Thomas Nelson and Sons Ltd 1990
ISBN 0–17–555896 5
NPN 9 8 7 6 5 4 3 2 1

Designed by DP Press, Sevenoaks, Kent

Printed and bound in Hong Kong

Contents

LIST OF LESSONS

Tense contrasts

1	Problem students	*Present simple or present continuous?*
2	Stop thief!	*Past simple or past continuous?*
3	European Community	*Past simple or present perfect?*
4	What have you been doing?	*Present perfect simple or present perfect continuous?*
5	Witness to crime	*Past simple or past perfect?*
6	Changes	*Used to do or be used to doing?*
7	We're going to have a good time!	*Ways of expressing the future (going to, will, present simple/ continuous)*

Modals

8	Sports day	*Can, could, be able to*
9	Signs of obligation	*Must, have to, should, don't have to, shouldn't*
10	You needn't worry	*Mustn't, needn't, don't have to*

Conditionals

11	If I were you . . .	*First and second conditionals*
12	If you hadn't . . .	*Third conditional*
13	What if . . .?	*Mixed conditionals*

Infinitive and –ing

14	Holiday experiences	*Verbs followed by infinitive or –ing*
15	Eyewitness	*Verbs of perception with the present participle/infinitive*

Verbs

16	Christmas presents	*Verbs with two objects*
17	Partners	*Stative and dynamic verbs*
18	Look it up!	*Phrasal verbs*
19	English is spoken here	*Passives*

Adjectives and adverbs

20	Hand of death	*–ed and –ing adjectives*
21	Describing objects	*Order of adjectives before a noun*
22	References	*Position of adverbs*

Prepositions/Clauses of Time

23	All in the home	*Prepositions of location*
24	Michael Jackson	*Prepositions of time (at, by, during, for, from ... till, in, on, since)*
25	An eventful day!	*Prepositions and adverbs of time (after, as, before, during, for, since, until, when, while)*

Articles

26	Can you count it?	*Countable and uncountable nouns*
27	This is the life!	*The use of the definite article*

Miscellaneous

28	A night at the movies	*Question tags*
29	Anyone for tennis?	*All, both, every, each, none, neither*
30	My secret desire	*Wish + would or wish + past simple?*

Introduction

BRIEF DESCRIPTION

Survival Lessons is a resource book of complete lesson plans comprising thirty lessons of photocopiable students' material with accompanying teacher's notes. All the material required for each lesson is contained within the two photocopiable pages. All the lessons are self-contained and may be used in any order. The lessons do not form a progressive course but are designed to be used in conjunction with a main course book. The lessons are based on structural problem areas and comprise four stages: an initial analysis (inductive); controlled practice; communication exercises; and a final test. Each lesson lasts between 45 and 60 minutes. The material is aimed at the intermediate/pre-Cambridge First Certificate level. Some of the structures are suitable for lower levels although the vocabulary may not be totally familiar to such classes. Students at the Cambridge First Certificate level may find the material useful for revision purposes.

BACKGROUND

Teachers often face two problems:

1 What to do when a lesson has to be taught without time for preparation.

2 How to deal with the persistent problem of repeated errors with particular structures when these structures have already been presented and practised in a main course.

This book has been designed to tackle these problems:

1 Everything the teacher needs for a 45–60 minute lesson is contained within the lesson plan. Access to a photocopier in order to make a copy of the lesson for each student is the only additional requirement. This will be useful for teachers taking substitution and for those with little preparation time or without access to cassette recorders, overhead projectors etc.

2 Each lesson is based on a particular grammar problem. These problems emerged from a survey of teachers of mixed nationality classes who were asked to list specific grammatical items or contrasts which most frequently caused repeated difficulties for their students.

METHODOLOGY AND UNIT DESIGN

It is assumed that students will be familiar with the grammar items covered in a particular lesson, but will have experienced difficulty or confusion over them. The lessons do not present new structures but begin with an inductive analysis section which enables the teacher to find out how much the students already know and helps the student to activate and build on his or her existing knowledge. The analysis sections are designed to highlight the potentially confusing contrasts between structures rather than the individual uses of grammar items (which are generally well covered in main courses). Areas of particular difficulty are explained in the teacher's notes, and teachers may, if they so wish, present these to those students who are unable to complete the analysis section themselves. The use of complex grammatical terminology has been kept to a

minimum but, where its use is unavoidable, a full explanation is given in the teacher's notes. In situations where students are not used to such terminology the teacher may wish to pre-teach the relevant terms during the analysis phase.

The second stage consists of controlled practice. Here students have the opportunity to work individually on traditional exercises designed to test accuracy in the use of the structures. Modern courses often feature a very rapid progression from presentation to free practice; this type of exercise gives the student a chance to consolidate and become familiar with the structure before moving to the third section which contains communicative activities.

These activities involve information gap, role play, games or simulated authentic tasks which require oral use of the structures in pairs or groups. The intention of this section is to enable the students to use the structures in an interactive situation within a realistic context, with the emphasis on fluent use of the forms for effective communication.

The final section is a test, designed so that students and their teachers may discover how far they have mastered the structures. Each test is marked out of ten so the students can record their scores and know whether further work is necessary. Suggestions for further practice are contained in the teacher's notes.

USING THE MATERIAL

Each lesson may be used in three ways:

1 *As a follow-up lesson.* Here the lesson can be integrated into a planned course, in conjunction with a course book. After presentation and practice in a course book, teachers may feel that further analysis, clarification and practice of a particular structure or contrast may be required. Grammar practice books are frequently used in this situation: **Survival Lessons** has the advantage that analysis and communicative practice are included, in addition to traditional accuracy exercises.

2 *As revision material.* Towards the end of a series of lessons, teachers will want to revise important structural items and to go through problems. Lessons from **Survival Lessons** can be selectively chosen to cover those areas required. The analysis and test sections can be used independently to check students' needs, and the material offers an opportunity to review problems and revise structural items while maintaining student interest and motivation by presenting the input and practice through new material rather than repeating lessons from main course books.

3 *As a one-off (e.g. substitution) lesson.* Each lesson is designed for minimum teacher preparation and maximum exploitation of the photocopiable material. Vocabulary level and content have been controlled so that the lessons can be taught at a variety of levels in the intermediate range. Selection of a suitable lesson and photocopying of the relevant pages are the only preparation required. Where preparation time is available, teachers will find that reading through the teacher's notes

accompanying each unit will facilitate successful use of the material. However, in a rushed situation, teachers may read through the notes while students are working on the analysis section. Notes on areas of grammatical difficulty and detailed instructions on exploitation of the communicative exercises are included in the teacher's section.

The answers to all closed exercises are contained in the teacher's notes accompanying each lesson.

FURTHER PRACTICE

At the end of most lesson plans suggestions are made for relevant further practice. The practice exercises come from five sources:

Active Grammar Exercises   D Adamson and D Cobb   Longman   1987   (*AGE*)
Basic Grammar Exercises   John Eastwood   OUP   1984   (*BEG*)
English Grammar in Use   Raymond Murphy   CUP   1985   (*EGU*)
Grammar and Practice   Jimmie Hill et al   LTP   1989   (*GP*)
Practising Grammar Workbooks 2 and 3   Jon Blundell   Nelson   1989/90   (*PG2/3*)

The initials in brackets are used as reference throughout. Although care has been taken to ensure the relevance of these exercises, inevitably some practise less or more than the unit in this book.

Problem students

Present simple or present continuous?

LESSON PLAN

Aim: To distinguish between and practise the use of the present simple tense for (1) permanent situations, (2) habits and repeated actions, (3) facts and general truths, and the use of the present continuous tense for (1) temporary situations and (2) actions happening now.

Topics: School reports, summer courses.

Lesson phases: Analysis and feedback 15 mins. Practice 15 mins.   Communication 15 mins.   Test 10 mins.   Total 55 mins.

A   ANALYSIS

Allow seven or eight minutes for each exercise.

1 Pre-teach vocabulary: *truancy*.
   Suggested answers:
   a Because her work isn't very good and she often misses lessons.
   b No, she enjoys some subjects.
   c Her mother has left home and her father expects Sandy to stay at home.
   d Elicit two or three suggestions from the class.

2 *Answers:*

	permanent situation	temporary situation	habit or repeated action	general truth or fact	action happening now
a					✓
b			✓		
c				✓	
d		✓			
e	✓				
f				✓	
g			✓		
h		✓			
	simple	*cont.*	*simple*	*simple*	*cont.*

B   PRACTICE

Allow six or seven minutes for each exercise.

3 *Answers:*
   a works, is studying
   b is staying
   c is
   d arrives
   e am trying
   f are singing
   g like, am not enjoying
   h keep

4 *Answers:*
   a My grandmother lives in a cottage. She has lived there all her life.
   b Statistics show that the Dutch are the tallest race.
   c I'm Spanish, I come from Madrid.
   d Look! That woman is trying to jump on the bus.
   e The state of Florida has a sub-tropical climate.

C   COMMUNICATION

Allow ten to fifteen minutes for the exercise.

5 Divide the class into pairs and nominate Students A and B in each pair. Ask the students to look at the Course Programme and check vocabulary. Students B should then look through their questionnaire while students A complete the Course Programme. When students A have completed the Programme they are ready to be interviewed by their partners.

D   TEST

Allow ten minutes for the test and checking.

6 *Answers:*
   a (i)   **b** (i)   **c** (ii)   **d** (i)   **e** (ii)
   f (i)   **g** (ii)   **h** (i)   **i** (i)   **j** (ii)

FURTHER PRACTICE

AGE   Ex 92
BEG   Exs 10, 11
GP   Ex 6.1

Stop thief!

Past simple or past continuous?

LESSON PLAN

Aim: To distinguish between the past simple and past continuous tenses, particularly with reference to interrupted actions, and particularly in order to be able to build a narrative.

Topics: Narratives about a car theft and a fire.

Lesson phases: Analysis and feedback 20 mins. Practice 10 mins. Communication 15 mins. Test 10 mins. Total 55 mins.

A ANALYSIS

The picture story is a pictorial representation of a simple narrative. The students have enough information in the gapped story to be able to supply the verbs and order the pictures. You might find it useful to ask the students to cut out the pictures and captions, once they have filled in the gaps, to make the ordering easier and to get a better sense of the continuity of the story. This is obviously dependent on your resources. Allow about ten minutes for the first two exercises so that there is plenty of time for the analysis.

1 *Answers:*
   a started/decided, noticed/saw, decided   **b** got, drove
   c parked, ran/went, forgot   **d** looked
   e ran   **f** paid, went
   g saw/noticed   **h** came/walked

2 *Answers:*
   a 3   **b** 8   **c** 5   **d** 2   **e** 6   **f** 1   **g** 7   **h** 4

3 The answers are in the captions.

4 *Answers:*

	examples	past simple	past cont.
Sequence of events in the past.	got, drove	✓	
Background information to a narrative	was pouring		✓
An action which interrupts another.	looked out of the window	✓	
An action which is interrupted by another.	was waiting to pay		✓
Two actions taking place at the same time.	was waiting to was looking out		✓

Which words can introduce an interrupted action? *as, while*
Which word can introduce an interrupting action? *when*

Note: An action in the past simple can also be introduced by *when*, but this action is usually given with another action in the past simple, to express simultaneity, e.g. *He left the room when I walked in.*

Your students may use different examples from the above in their analysis. Allow any that are correct. It might be necessary to do this analysis with the students as it is quite complicated.

B PRACTICE

Allow only ten minutes for this section as it is fairly simple and should cause no problems.

5 *Answers:*
   The verbs here are only suggestions. Allow any suitable verbs.

   a was doing, heard
   b finished, went
   c was falling, were wearing
   d broke, was running
   e finished, were playing, left, went, met
   f was driving, was rehearsing

6 *Answers:*
   a 2   **b** 4   **c** 5   **d** 3   **e** 1

C COMMUNICATION

7 This exercise gives practice in the two tenses examined here and in forming a narrative using past tenses. The students work in pairs with half a picture story each, which they have to put together orally. As in the analysis section, if you have scissors to hand, it might be easier for the students to cut out the pictures. Follow this procedure:

   ● Tell the students to divide into pairs, A and B.
   ● Each student looks at the relevant pictures and makes notes about the story in each picture. Ensure that they are aware of the need to use the two past tenses.
   ● Each student describes his/her picture to his/her partner in narrative form. Monitor for use of the tenses and for narrative form. Ensure that they are using *I*.
   ● From the descriptions, the pairs order the pictures.
   ● They then retell the story as a complete narrative.
   ● Ask one or two pairs to tell their stories to the class; the other students correct.
   ● The students could write up the story, or write a similar story, for homework.

D TEST

Allow about ten minutes for the students to do the test and for it to be marked in the class. The score is out of ten.

8 *Answers:*
   a was making, was watching
   b fell, shattered
   c was crossing, hit
   d was dawning, were singing
   e was having, disturbed

FURTHER PRACTICE

AGE	Ex 97
EGU	Exs 12.3, 12.4
GP	Exs 9.1–9.8
PG2	Unit 8, Exs 5–7

European Community

Past simple or present perfect?

LESSON PLAN

Aims: To compare and practise the use of the present perfect and past simple tenses as follows:

Past simple: an action or situation in the past where the exact time is given.

Present perfect: an action or situation in the past when either the action or the situation or the time period is still continuing;
an action or situation which started in the past and finished very recently;
a series of repeated actions in the past which may continue into the present.

Also to practise the use of adverbials with the present perfect tense: *yet, already, just, since, for.*

Topic: The European Community, office tasks.

Lesson phases: Analysis and feedback 20 mins. Practice 10 mins. Communication 15 mins. Test 5 mins. Total 50 mins.

A   ANALYSIS

Allow ten minutes for this section and ten minutes for checking and feedback.

1   Incorrect sentences are **c**, **d**, **f**, and **g**.

2   *Answers:*

	which sentences	*present perfect*	*past simple*
A an action or situation in the past where the exact time is given	a, h		✓
B an action or situation in the past when either the action of the situation or the time period is still continuing (this can also refer to a negative action or situation)	b, e	✓	
C an action or situation which started in the past and finished very recently	i	✓	
D a series of repeated actions in the past which may continue into the present	j	✓	

B   PRACTICE

Allow ten minutes for this section.
(The 'category' of each sentence is given in brackets: refer students to the categories in exercises 2 if they experience difficulties.)

3   *Answers:*
  a Ireland has been a member of the EEC since 1973. (B)
  b I have never visited Paris but I went to Versailles last year. (B)(A)
  c British Airways has just announced a new fare to Moscow. (C)
  d Peter hasn't finished his homework yet. (B)
  e Has Maria ever seen a bullfight? (B)/
       Did Maria ever see a bullfight? (American usage)

4   *Answers:*
  I opened the mail at half past nine.
  I took the parcels to the post office before coffee time.
  I made coffee for the secretaries at 11 o'clock.
  I took the new fax machine to the basement at 2 o'clock.
  (All type A)
  I've (already) bought 100 envelopes.
  I haven't bought a birthday card for Julie (yet).
  I haven't replaced the light bulbs in the reception area (yet).
  I've (already) collected the pay cheques from Mr Griffiths.
  (All type B)

C   COMMUNICATION

5   Allow ten minutes for pairs to complete the questionnaire and five minutes for pairs to compare results and complete the discussion task.

D   TEST

Allow five minutes.

6   *Answers:*
  a (ii) (type A)   **b** (i) (type C)   **c** (ii) (type B)
  d (ii) (type B)   **e** (ii) (type B)   **f** (iii) (type B)
  g (i) (type A)   **h** (ii) (type B)   **i** (iii) (type D)
  j (i) (type B)

FURTHER PRACTICE

AGE   Ex 101
BEG   Exs 19, 20
GP   Exs 14.3, 14.4, 14.7

What have you been doing?

Present perfect simple or present perfect continuous?

LESSON PLAN

Aim: To distinguish between the uses of the present perfect simple and the present perfect continuous, particularly looking at the emphasis on the result of the action with the simple and the duration of the action with the continuous. There are other possible interpretations of the differences, but for the purposes of this unit these have been simplified.

Topics: Activities, especially leisure activities.

Lesson phases: Analysis and feedback 20 mins. Practice 10 mins. Communication 20 mins. Test 10 mins. Total 60 minutes.

A ANALYSIS

The six drawings contrast the uses of the present perfect simple and the present perfect continuous. The uses examined here are:

- present perfect simple to focus on the result of an action and the number of times an action has been done;
- present perfect continuous to focus on the action itself and its duration.

The uses have been simplified here and for a more in-depth treatment, you should refer to a grammar book.

1 *Answers:*
 a 2 **b** 4 **c** 5 **d** 3 **e** 1 **f** 6

2 *Answers:*
 a c 5 **b** a 2 **c** e 1 **d** f 6 **e** b 4 **f** d 3

3 The analysis here concentrates only on the sentences in exercise 1 (the captions) so as not to confuse with the questions.
 Answers:
 Duration d; Result a,f; Number b
 The other two captions, c and e, focus on the action itself.

4 *Answers:*
 a When we want to focus on the action itself, we use the *present perfect continuous.*
 b When we want to focus on the result of the action, we use the *present perfect simple.*
 c When we want to focus on the duration of the action, we use the *present perfect continuous.*
 d When we want to focus on the number of times the action has been done, we use the *present perfect simple.*

Here are some further contrasts to give your students if there are any problems.
I've been knocking on your door for five minutes! (duration)
I've knocked at least ten times! (number)
Have you had a good morning?
 Yes, I've been sunbathing. (action)
Mmm. You look quite red.
 I know, I've stayed in the sun for too long. (result)

B PRACTICE

If the students have understood the differences, they should only need about ten minutes for this section.

5 This exercise focuses on the duration/number distinction.
 Answers:
 a for half an hour **b** at least twice/ten times
 c for half an hour **d** at least twice/ten times
 e at least twice/ten times **f** for half an hour/for days
 g for days **h** at least twice/ten times

6 This exercise is in two parts. Ask the students to do the matching first, then to fill in the verbs.
 Answers:
 Matching: **a** 3 **b** 1 **c** 5 **d** 2 **e** 4
 Verbs:
 a been studying at* **d** been staying in*
 b taken **e** bought/taken
 c had/drunk

* If the students use *been at/in*, allow it, as it is correct English, and explain that some verbs, such as *to be*, rarely take a continuous form.

C COMMUNICATION

7 This is a question and answer exercise, conducted in pairs, which practises the two tenses. Allow about five minutes for the students to look through the form, and fifteen for the pairwork. Encourage the students to use their imagination when answering the questions and if possible, to apply them to their own interests and to add/think of more details (for example, which language they have been studying). Follow this procedure:

- Ask the students to look through the form.
- Divide the students into pairs, A and B.
- Ask Student A in each pair to start interviewing Student B. Make sure they understand the situation and explain *market researcher*. Encourage a variety of questions, such as:
 How long have you been a member?
 Have you been using the fitness studio?
 How frequently/how many times have you used it?
 Have you been studying a language?
 Which one have you been studying? etc.
 This is the first active use of questions in this unit and you may wish to revise the form first.
- Monitor the students' use of the tenses and check that A is writing the information down.
- If you have time, ask the students to swap roles and repeat the interview.
- The students could write up the market research results for homework.

D TEST

8 Allow about ten minutes for the test. Give half a mark for each correct (or suitable) verb and half for each correct tense in the table. Give the students a score out of ten.
 Answers:
 a **pps** been to/visited **b** **pps** been to/seen/attended
 c **ppc** been drinking **d** **ppc** been studying/working
 e **pps** seen/been to/watched **f** **ppc** been playing
 g **pps** eaten **h** **pps** beaten **i** **pps** given/prescribed
 j **ppc** been sleeping/feeling

FURTHER PRACTICE

EGU Exs 17.1, 17.3
GP Ex 13.4
PG3 Unit 1, Exs 4-6

Witness to crime

Past simple or past perfect?

LESSON PLAN

Aim: To distinguish between and practise the use of the past simple and past perfect tenses with particular attention to their use to show the sequence of events in the past.

Topics: Witnessing crime, alibis.

Lesson phases: Analysis and feedback 15 mins. Practice 10 mins. Communication 15 mins. Test 10 mins. Total 50 mins.

A ANALYSIS

Allow eight or nine minutes for exercise 1 and six or seven minutes for exercise 2.

1 Pre-teach vocabulary: *witness, statement, to be tied up, safe* (noun), *electronic alarm*.
Discuss the first question with the class. *Suggested answer:* Ms Wesley.
Answer to sequence exercise:
1 e 2 b 3 f 4 h 5 a 6 d 7 g 8 i 9 c

2 *Answers:*

	past simple	past perfect
a To talk about something which happened at a specific time in the past. e.g. *I returned home at 5 o'clock.*	✓	
b To talk about something which happened at a specific time in the past but before something else in the past. e.g. *earlier that morning Ms Wesley had come into my office.*		✓
c To talk about something which happened at an unspecified time in the past before something else in the past. e.g. *I knew something was wrong because the lock on the front door had been broken.*		✓

B PRACTICE

Allow five minutes for each exercise.

3 *Answers:*
a (i) **b** (i) **c** (ii) **d** (i) **e** (ii)

4 *Answers:*
a I arrived after the shop had closed.
b I bought my first car after I had passed the driving test.
c When we sold our house we bought a farm.
d I started working after I had graduated from college.
e When Jim finished eating dessert the waiter brought the bill.

C COMMUNICATION

5 Allow five minutes to introduce the game and for pairs to prepare their alibis. The questioning activity should be limited to one or two minutes per 'suspect' – the time this takes will depend on the size of the class. Follow this procedure:

- Explain the meaning of 'alibi' and read through the instructions with the class.
- Make sure that each pair invents two or three different activities for their alibi, e.g. *We had a pizza between 6 and 6.30, we then went to the cinema from 6.30 to 8.30, and we had coffee from 8.30 to 9 o'clock.*
- Remind them that the other students will be able to ask them about any detail of their alibi, e.g. *What were you wearing? Did you sit at the front or the back of the cinema? Where had you been before you had a pizza?*
- When all the pairs have discussed their alibis, ask one student to come to the front of the class. His or her partner must wait outside while the class questions the student.
- You may need to suggest questions to the class if they have not played this game before (see above).
- After a minute or so ask the student to step outside and invite his or her partner back in to be questioned. The task of the class now is to find any inconsistencies between their alibis by asking detailed questions.
- Repeat the process until every student has been questioned or until an obvious 'murderer' emerges.

D TEST

Allow ten minutes for completion of the test and checking.

6 *Answers:*
a When I arrived home the TV was missing. Someone had stolen it.
b I was late for the flight. When I arrived it had already left.
c Joyce is still hungry, even though she ate a big lunch.
d I didn't know the man. I had never seen him before.
e Ann didn't want to visit the theatre because she had seen the play already.
f Mrs Greville returned to work after her children had grown up.
g I'm feeling rather tired because I stayed up very late last night.
h Jimmy was nervous when he visited the dentist because he had had two fillings on his previous visit.
i When I returned to the hotel my room looked much tidier because the maid had made the bed.
j I'm starving! I didn't have any breakfast this morning.

FURTHER PRACTICE

EGU Ex 22.4
PG3 Unit 3, Exs 3–4

Changes

Used to do or be used to doing?

LESSON PLAN

Aim: To show the difference between the past simple and *used to*, and between *used to do* and *be used to doing*.

Topics: Changes in lifestyle.

Lesson phases: Analysis and feedback 25 mins. Practice 10 mins. Communication 15 mins. Test 10 mins. Total 60 mins.

A   ANALYSIS

Allow about fifteen minutes for the students to do the first four exercises and about ten minutes for discussion.

1   The answers to this should be obvious from the activities involved. Ask the students to do this before they read the dialogue.

Answers: Past   1, 4, 6, 7
Present   2, 3, 5, 8

2   The students read the dialogue and then match the phrases with their meanings by drawing lines.

Answers:

a I used to be handsome.	**5** continuous state in the past
b I used to play a lot of sport.	**4** repeated action in the past
c I robbed a bank.	**1** single action in the past
d I'm used to being in this cell.	**3** continuous state in the present
e I'm used to doing ten minutes exercise every day.	**2** repeated action in the present

Note If your students do not know the meanings of *state* and *habit*, explain them before this exercise is tackled.

3   Here the students are asked to provide the grammatical ways of expressing the following.

Answers:

a single action in the past	past simple
b repeated action in the past	*used to* + infinitive
c continuous state in the past	*used to* + infinitive (often *be* or *have*)
d continuous state in the present	*be used to* + *–ing*
e repeated action in the present	*be used to* + *–ing*

Note Make sure the students are aware that the *be used to + –ing* form is not the most normal way of expressing these concepts in the present, but that they have a suggestion of having become accustomed to the state or action.

4   *Answers:*

a F   He used to go out with his wife and children.
b T
c F   He is used to being in a cell.
d F   He used to play a lot of sport.
e F   He didn't use to spend a lot of time reading on his own./He's used to spending a lot of time reading on his own.
f T

Ask the students to do just the true/false exercise first, then the correction. Point out the form of the negative *didn't use to*.

B   PRACTICE

These two exercises should only take about ten minutes.

5   *Answers:*

a used to go out	**b** is used to living
c is used to playing	**d** used to lead
e used to have	**f** is used to eating
g is used to watching	**h** used to be

6   *Answers:*

a When he was free, Barry used to do a lot of exercise, but now he's used to doing very little.
b When I was a child I used to ride a bicycle but now I'm used to driving a car.
c When my brother was in the army he used to get up very early but now he's used to lying in bed late in the morning.
d When I was at school I used to do my homework in the evenings but now I'm used to watching television in the evenings.

This exercise is intended as a contrast of the two forms. If you find it too contrived, ask the students to produce the past form of *used to* only in the second clause.

C   COMMUNICATION

7   This exercise is intended as a guessing game which focuses on the meaning difference between the two structures. Follow this procedure:

• Divide the class into groups of four or five.
• Ask each student to write the four sentences as in the model, without showing them to any of the other students. In case they have difficulty in thinking of situations, here are some prompts:
   – you have won a lot of money in a competition
   – you have left school/college and have got a very demanding job
   – you have moved to a different country
   – you have passed your driving test
   – you were blind and you have received your sight back.
• Ask the students to read their sentences out to their groups. The rest of the group guesses the change in situation, and can ask more *used to do/be used to doing* questions if they wish.

D   TEST

The test should only take a few minutes. Give the students a score out of ten.

8   *Answers:*

a didn't use to have   **b** used to work
c are used to studying   **d** didn't use to be
e are used to travelling   **f** used to live
g didn't use to move   **h** used to be
i used to die   **j** are used to getting/receiving

FURTHER PRACTICE

EGU   Ex 62.3
GP   Exs 38.3, 38.6, 39.2, 39.3

We're going to have a good time!

Ways of expressing the future

LESSON PLAN

Aims: To compare and contrast the usage and meaning of the most common ways of expressing the future at this level. Those ways are present continuous, *will*, *going to* and present simple.

Topic: Holidays.

Lesson phases: Analysis and feedback 30 mins. Practice 10 mins. Communication 10 mins. Test 10 mins. Total 60 mins.

A   ANALYSIS

This unit looks at four ways of expressing the future and their usages: the future simple (*will*) for predictions and spontaneous decisions; *going to* for intention and prediction based on firm evidence in the present; present continuous for firm plans and arrangements; and the present simple for timetables and schedules. The future perfect and future continuous are not addressed as they are felt to be beyond the scope of this book.

1   *Answers:*
   a She's going to stay there all afternoon.
   b She says that Cathy will get bored.
   c They are having dinner with two boys.
   d She says it will be warmer than the sea.
   e She thinks it's going to rain because of the clouds.
   f She decides to go to buy some sun oil.

2   *Answers:*
   intention to do something   **1**
   a decision made at the time of speaking   **5, 9**
   an arrangement already made   **3, 4**
   a prediction about someone/something   **2, 6**
   a statement about the future based on evidence in the present   **7, 8**
   something on a timetable/schedule   **10**

3   *Answers:*

	expresses	*will*	*pres. cont.*	*going to*	*pres. simple*
1 I'm going to stay here ...	intention			✓	
2 you'll get bored ...	prediction	✓			
3 ... we're having dinner . . .	arrangement		✓		
4 We're meeting them at half past eight ...	arrangement		✓		
5 I think I'll have a swim.	sp. dec.*	✓			
6 The pool will be warmer ...	prediction	✓			
7 I'm going to get burnt.	pres. evid.†			✓	
8 I think it's going to rain.	pres. evid.			✓	
9 I'll go and get some.	sp. dec.	✓			
10 The bus leaves at five thirty.	schedule				✓

B   PRACTICE

These are two simple exercises and should need only a few minutes if the students have understood the distinctions. In some cases other answers may be possible, for example, the present continuous and *going to* futures are often used interchangeably by native speakers, but the ones suggested here are those the students should reach according to the analysis given in this unit.

4   There are two cases here where the future continuous could also be used (d and e). If your students know it and use it, accept it as correct.
   Answers:
   a are spending
   b are staying
   c will keep
   d are going to sunbathe
   e are going to try out
   f are sailing
   g leaves
   h will be
   i won't be
   j won't be

5   This exercise is quite open-ended: some suggested answers are given below, but others are possible.
   Answers:
   a I'll put that up for you!
   b Be careful! The chair's going to break!
   c No, I'm visiting my parents during that week.
   d It leaves at three-thirty.
   e You'll meet a beautiful girl.
   f I'm going to buy a car.

C   COMMUNICATION

This is a straightforward exercise and shouldn't need too much time. Allow about ten minutes only.

6   Give the students a couple of minutes to think about the questions. Then in groups of four they discuss them. Encourage the students to use their imagination and to think while they are talking; they should then change future tenses quite naturally.

D   TEST

7   Allow ten minutes for the test and give the students a score out of ten.
   Answers:
   a (ii) **b** (i) **c** (iii) **d** (i) **e** (iii) **f** (i) **g** (ii) **h** (iii) **i** (i) **j** (ii)

FURTHER PRACTICE

BEG   Ex 34
EGU   Exs 4.3, 5.4, 6.1
GP   Ex 17.8

*spontaneous decision
† present evidence

Sports day

Can, could, be able to

LESSON PLAN

Aims: To contrast and practise ways of expressing possibility, ability and permission in the past, present and future, using *can* and *be able to*.

Topic: School sports day, sports.

Lesson phases: Analysis and feedback 25 mins. Practice 10 mins. Communication 15 mins. Test 5 mins. Total 55 mins.

A   ANALYSIS

This section looks at the different uses of *can* and *could*: for permission, ability and possibility; and at the use of *be able to* for the future of *can*, as well as with the meaning of *manage to*. Allow the students time to read the dialogues and do the analysis exercises before going on to the practice.

1   The answers here naturally use the modals and help to focus the students' minds on their uses.

Answers:
a No, she can't, because she's going to visit her grandmother on that day.
b Because she can swim very well.
c Yes, it was great.
d Someone from the other school won the swimming and Alison wasn't able to keep up.
e She thinks he can run well.
f He didn't win because he was only able to finish third.

2   *Answers:*
permission (or lack of) 2, 3
possibility (or lack of) 1, 7, 8
ability (or inability) 4, 5, 6, 9, 10,11

the present 4, 5, 6, 10
the future 1, 2, 3, 7
the past 8, 9, 11

We express possibility in the future with *will be able to* (but we use *can/can't* to express permission in the future). Numbers 9 and 11 express that someone tried very hard; this is expressed by *be able to.*

3   *Answers:*
Is it possible that . . .?   Can you . . .
I don't have the ability to . . .   I can't . . .
I don't have permission to . . .   I can't . . .
He just managed to . . .   He was just able to . . .

4   *Answers:*
a 9 b 5 c 10 d 2 e 8 f 6 g 11 h 3 i 7 j 4 k 1

B   PRACTICE

Allow only about ten minutes for these exercises as they are fairly simple.

5   *Answers:*
a can b can't/won't be able to (both are acceptable)
c could, can d was able to e can't f couldn't, can't
g can't h will be able to

6   The answers below are suggestions, as several different answers are possible here.

Answers:
a Can we stay at home tonight?
b You can't buy that.
c I can't sing now, though I could when I was younger.
d I wasn't able to contact you, however hard I tried.
e If you come to stay we'll be able to visit all the sights.

C   COMMUNICATION

7   Allow about fifteen minutes for this exercise, and encourage students to use their imagination. Give the class a few minutes to read and think about their roles, then allow them a few minutes to decide on the weekend and on what they can do to make it special. If you have time, ask pairs to check what they have decided with other pairs. Follow this procedure:

- Give the class a few minutes to read and think about their roles and think about the things they can/can't do.
- Tell them to decide which weekend is possible and what they can do to make it special.
- Monitor for use of the structures.
- Ask some of the better pairs to tell the class their plans.

D   TEST

Allow five minutes only for this test as it is very short, then mark it and give your students a score out of ten.

8   *Answers:*
a could b couldn't c couldn't d could e was able to
f could g can h can't i will be able to j won't be able to

FURTHER PRACTICE

AGE   Ex 123
BEG   Ex 39
EGU   Ex 26.4

Signs of obligation
Must, have to, should, don't have to, shouldn't

LESSON PLAN

Aims: To contrast and practise ways of expressing advice and obligation, using *must, have to* and *should*.

Topics: Rules and regulations, youth hostelling.

Lesson phases: Analysis and feedback 20 mins. Practice 15 mins. Communication 15 mins. Test 5 mins. Total 55 mins.

A ANALYSIS

Allow about twenty minutes for these exercises and feedback.

1 This exercise is a simple familiarisation task with the language to be analysed. The illustrations are all signs or speech bubbles containing the modal verbs.

   Answers:
   1 park **2** doctor's surgery **3** airport **4** instruction manual **5** hotel **6** shop **7** doctor's surgery **8** airport **9** park **10** shop

2 *Answers:*
   The students should underline the modal verbs:
   1 must **2** should **3** do not have to **4** must not **5** have to **6** must **7** shouldn't **8** must not **9** shouldn't **10** don't have to

3 This exercise looks at the meanings of the modal verbs. The students have to identify their purpose and in which notices each appears. For the purpose of this unit *must* and *have to* are treated as having the same meaning, i.e. obligation to do something. If you wish to differentiate between them, the distinction most commonly made is that of *must* expressing an obligation imposed by the speaker, and *have to* expressing an obligation imposed by someone other than the speaker, often by authority. You could add this to the analysis by asking the students which type of obligation is expressed each time it appears.

   Answers:

	verbs	examples
obligation to do something (two ways of expressing this)	must have to	1, 6 5
obligation not to do something	must not	4, 8
no obligation to do something	do not have to	3, 10
advice to do something	should	2
advice not to do something	shouldn't	7, 9

B PRACTICE

Allow about fifteen minutes for these practice exercises and for checking.

Note: The analysis section did not look at questions using the modal verbs as that may cause confusion. However, questions are included here for practice, and if your students are relatively unfamiliar with modal verbs you may need to introduce the question forms before doing these exercises.

4 *Answers:*
   a Everyone must remove their shoes on entry.
   b You should take malaria pills but you must have the typhoid inoculation.
   c Do we really have to book a table at this restaurant?
   d We really mustn't give you that information.
   e Women shouldn't wear short skirts in this country.
   f Do I have to pay for the course in advance and should I buy the books before I start?

5 *Answers:*
   These are suggested answers only; there are other possibilities. Encourage your students to vary the answers as much as possible.
   1 You mustn't bring dogs in here.
   2 You have to go through here if you have goods to declare.
   3 This item should/must be dry cleaned.
   4 You don't have to change if you are going to Leeds.
   5 You mustn't smoke here.
   6 You should eat less fat, sugar and alcohol./You shouldn't eat so much fat, sugar and alcohol.
   7 You should wash this item by hand; you don't have to have it dry cleaned. You should not iron it.
   8 You have to leave the train here.

C COMMUNICATION

Allow about fifteen minutes for this exercise.

6 This exercise practises forming questions and answering them using the verbs above. You might like to allocate the B role to students who are weak at forming questions. Follow this procedure:

   ● Divide the students into pairs and allocate the roles.
   ● Ask Students A to read through the rules together and to make sure they understand them. If you have a good class, you could ask them to make up a few other rules according to what they know about youth hostelling.
   ● Ask Students B to read through their information and to formulate the questions. They could think of a few more questions if they have time. Allow only five minutes for this stage.
   ● Tell the students that they should do the role play in pairs, and that the questioners should make notes of the answers.
   ● The students do the role play. Monitor for correct use of the modals.

D TEST

Allow only five minutes for this test and give your students scores out of ten.

7 *Answers:*
   a don't have to **b** should **c** mustn't **d** have to **e** shouldn't **f** Must **g** do I have to **h** mustn't **i** don't have to **j** shouldn't

FURTHER PRACTICE

AGE Ex 127
EGU Ex 32.1

You needn't worry

Mustn't, needn't, don't have to

LESSON PLAN

Aim: To distinguish between and practise the use of the modal verb forms *mustn't, needn't* and *don't have to.*

Topics: Legal advice concerning renting or buying property, travel restrictions.

Lesson phases: Analysis and feedback 15 mins. Practice 10 mins. Communication 15 mins. Test 10 mins. Total 50 mins.

A ANALYSIS

Allow 15 minutes.

1 Pre-teach vocabulary: *rent, landlord, to evict/eviction, court.*

Answers:
a No.
b No.
c No.

EVICTION PROCEDURES

LANDLORD'S OBLIGATIONS:
1. The landlord must give one month's notice in writing.
2. The landlord *has to get a court order.*

TENANT'S OBLIGATIONS:
1. The tenant must continue *to pay the rent.*
2. The tenant must leave when the court order is received.

---

2 *Answers:*

something	lack of obligation	obligation not to do
mustn't		✓
needn't	✓	
don't have to	✓	

What is the difference between *needn't* and *don't have to?* There is no difference in meaning although we usually use *don't have to* for impersonal lack of obligation (to do with outside authority, laws and rules) and *needn't* for personal lack of obligation (to do with private wishes, advice etc.). In most situations the two forms are interchangeable.

B PRACTICE

Allow seven or eight minutes for each exercise.

3 *Answers:*
a needn't b needn't c mustn't d mustn't
e mustn't f needn't g mustn't h mustn't

4 *Suggested answers:*
a *Visas:* Tourists don't have to get a visa if they stay for less than one month.
b *Currency:* Tourists mustn't take Ruzanian pesos out of the country.
c *Vaccination:* Tourists don't have to have vaccinations although they are recommended.
d *Duty Free Allowances:* Tourists don't have to make a declaration if they import duty free goods to the value of US$200.
e *Special Restrictions:* Tourists mustn't take photographs in the military zone.
Tourists mustn't import any weapons.

C COMMUNICATION

Allow fifteen minutes for completion of the role play exercise.

5 Pre-teach vocabulary: *solicitor, building insurance, deposit, contract (of sale), to borrow, to inspect, surveyor.*

Divide the class into pairs and nominate students A and B in each pair. Check that students only look at their own information box.

D TEST

Allow ten minutes for the test and checking.

6 *Answers:*
a You don't have to bring your passport.
b Children mustn't smoke cigarettes.
c Applicants don't have to bring an example of their work.
d You needn't give me a lift.
e Passengers mustn't stand during take-off.
f Guests mustn't smoke in the bedrooms.
g You needn't bring an umbrella.
h Tourists mustn't enter the naval base.
i You needn't bring me any books.
j Experienced swimmers don't have to attend the class.

FURTHER PRACTICE

AGE   Ex 128
EGU   Exs 32.4, 33.2
GP   Exs 35.1, 35.4, 35.5

If I were you . . .

First and second conditionals

LESSON PLAN

Aim: To illustrate the more common forms of the first and second conditionals and to compare and contrast the two.

Topic: Problems and dilemmas.

Lesson phases: Analysis and feedback 20 mins. Practice 10 mins. Communication 15 mins. Test 10 mins. Total 55 minutes.

A ANALYSIS

This section puts the common forms of these conditionals into context and then asks the students to analyse the types of conditional. The types examined here are:

if + present, present – for general truths and something which often happens

if + present, will – for something which is likely to happen

if + past, would – for something which is unlikely to happen, for something which cannot be true or is known to be untrue.

Allow about fifteen minutes for the exercises and then about five minutes for checking/discussion.

1 *Answers:*
The sequence is 1, 11, 2, 8, 3, 10, 4, 7, 5, 9, 6.

2 *Answers:*
a phones, gets **b** stayed, 'd go **c** get, 'll have **d** were, 'd talk **e** refuses, postpone **f** postponed, would be **g** were, would be **h** start, go on

3 This exercise uses the sentences from exercise 2 for the students to fill in a chart of the features of the different conditionals. This exercise would be a lot easier if the students could cut out and piece together the dialogue, as it contains clues to help the students with the chart, and these clues often appear in the speeches before or after the conditional sentence. After the students have done it, discuss the answers.

Answers:

	sentence number	present + present	present + will	past + would
something: which cannot be true	d, g			✓
likely to happen	c, e	✓	✓	✓
unlikely to happen	b, f			✓
generally true, or which often happens	a, h	✓		

The difference between **e** and the others is that it is an imperative, therefore using the present form of the infinitive.

B PRACTICE

This section should only take about ten minutes.

4 The students may give different answers to some of these questions, depending on their interpretation. The most likely answer is given, with alternaives where applicable in brackets.
a heat, boils – general truth
b 'll be sick, eat – likely to happen
c watered, 'd grow/survive – unlikely to happen on present evidence
d 'll keep/stay, take/get – likely to happen (keep, take/get – general truth)
e 'd buy the necklace, had – known not to be true
f woke up, 'd catch the train/might catch the train – unlikely

Note The exercises in this unit do not specifically address the use of modals with the conditionals, like the one in **f** above, nor do they address negatives and interrogatives specifically. You might wish to revise these aspects at the same time as doing these exercises. It is also worth noting for this exercise the position of the 'if' clause, and the use of the comma.

5 *Answers:*
a 4 **b** 6 **c** 1 **d** 3 **e** 2 **f** 5

C COMMUNICATION

Allow about five minutes for the pairwork here and a further ten minutes for the groupwork. Point out if necessary the use of *if + present, present* for the general conditions here; it suggests in questions **a**, **c** and **e** that these are situations which arise fairly commonly, while the use of the *if + past, would* conditional suggests that questions **b**, **d** and **f** are less likely to happen.

6 Follow this procedure:
- Divide the class into pairs and tell them to read through the questions quickly, agreeing on a course of action if possible.
- Encourage the students in this phase to write their answers in the short form of the conditional, e.g. for **b** *I'd call the police.*
- Tell the groups to join with another pair and to read through their responses, justifying them as much as possible as they go. The groups try to reach agreement about the response.
- Monitor to check use of the conditionals. Any groups that finish quickly can think of other questions.
- If you have time, throw the discussions to the whole class, and encourage other 'dilemma' questions.

D TEST

Allow about ten minutes for the students to do the test and for class checking. Give half a mark for each correct verb/tense, giving a maximum total of ten.

7 *Answers:*
a is, 'll go (will go) **b** wouldn't wear, was/were
c arrived, would faint **d** grow, put
e speak, ignore **f** speaks, 'll resign
g would find, had **h** become, feel
i forgot, would go **j** don't pay, phones

FURTHER PRACTICE

No further practice for this unit.

If you hadn't . . .

Third conditional

LESSON PLAN

Aim: To make students aware of the usage of the third conditional and to practise it.

Topic: Hypothesising about the past.

Lesson phases: Analysis and feedback 25 mins. Practice 10 mins. Communication 10 mins. Test 10 mins. Total 55 mins.

A ANALYSIS

This sequence of exercises is intended to help students understand the concept of the third conditional and how this relates to its formation. The picture story sets the scene and sets up the situation where a third conditional sentence is immediately understandable. The highlighting of the verbs in exercise 1 is to help the students with the formation of the past perfect and modal perfect in the third conditional. This unit does not look at variations of the conditional, using *might* etc. but encourage your students to use this if they already know it. The exercises in the Analysis section should take about fifteen to twenty minutes, with a few minutes left for discussion and feedback.

1 *Answers:*
The order is shown by the figure after the verb.

a trod 4		**b** asked 2		**c** shouted 6
d – 1		**e** rushed 5		**f** dropped 3
g braked, hit 7	**h** – 8			

Answers:

a Fred braked hard.	[T]
b Fred didn't brake hard.	[F]
c They had an accident.	[T]
d They didn't have an accident.	[F]

Draw the students' attention to the fact that the negative constructions in the third conditional refer to the fact that these actions really happened. Sally is purely hypothesising about a situation which is not true.

3 This exercise looks further at the positive/negative relationship in third conditionals.
true facts

John came.: c, d.	It was a good party.: b, d.
John didn't come.: a, b.	It wasn't a good party.: a, c.

B PRACTICE

The two practice exercises are quite straightforward and should only take about ten minutes if the students have understood the concept and can manipulate tenses easily.

4 *Answers:*

Sally	hadn't braked, wouldn't have had
Fred	hadn't shouted, wouldn't have braked
Sally	hadn't rushed*, wouldn't have shouted
Fred	hadn't trodden, wouldn't have rushed
Sally	hadn't dropped, wouldn't have trodden
Fred	hadn't asked, wouldn't have dropped
Fred	hadn't asked, wouldn't have had

* A past perfect continuous would be natural here. Allow your students to use one if they wish.

Point out that this exercise uses all negative constructions. If you have time, ask your students to change some of the sentences to use positive constructions, for example: *If you had braked more gently, we would have avoided an accident/we wouldn't have had the accident.*

5 *Answers:*

  a If I hadn't been tired, I wouldn't have had the accident.
  b If my friend hadn't seen the tree, he would have skied into it/he would have had a nasty accident.
  c If I had seen the broken glass on the ground, I wouldn't have trodden on it.
  d I would have shouted if I had seen the cat.
  e If the ambulance hadn't come quickly, it wouldn't have saved my life/I would have died/my life wouldn't have been saved.
  f If I had had* any insurance for the holiday, I wouldn't have had to pay the doctor's bills.

*Point out the use of *had had*, and the fact that it is perfectly acceptable English.

It is worth pointing out that we use commas in conditionals when the 'if clause' comes first, to separate the clauses, but not usually when the main clause comes first. In short sentences the comma may be omitted.

C COMMUNICATION

This exercise, to be done in pairs, practises the formation of third conditional questions and responses. For classes/pairs who are weak at forming the third conditional, encourage the use of full questions and responses, e.g. *If you had lived in Roman times, what would you have eaten? If I had lived in Roman times, I would have eaten grapes* etc. If the class has a reasonable grasp of the conditional, encourage the use of the more natural shorter forms, e.g. *If you had lived in Roman times, what would you have eaten? I'd have eaten grapes. And what would you have drunk?* etc.
Note: Encourage the use of contractions in this exercise.

6 Follow this procedure:

- Make sure the students understand the exercise; allocate the pairs and ask them to think about the topics given and others if possible.
- Illustrate the question form and the short answer form if necessary.
- Give the students a few minutes to ask and answer questions, then check the language by getting them to report back to the class, or to discuss in groups of four.

D TEST

7 Allow only ten minutes for the test. Give scores out of ten: one mark for each correct verb.
  a wouldn't have been, hadn't kicked
  b had lived, would have danced
  c Would . . . have visited, hadn't sent
  d would have got, hadn't given
  e hadn't won, wouldn't have bought/had won, would have bought

FURTHER PRACTICE

AGE	Ex 66
BEG	Ex 72
EGU	Exs 38.1, 38.2
GP	Ex 69.5
PG3	Unit 14, Exs 5–7

What if . . .?
Mixed conditionals

LESSON PLAN

Aim: To compare and contrast the first, second, third and mixed conditionals and to practise their use.

Topic: No overall topic area.

Lesson phases: Analysis and feedback 15 mins. Practice 15 mins. Communication 15 mins. Test 10 mins. Total 55 mins.

A   ANALYSIS

Allow about five minutes for each exercise.

1   *Answers:*
   a Carol
   b Mrs Beaton
   c Mr Beaton
   d Steve

2   *Answers:*
   a (i)   The car breaks down quite often. [T]
      (ii)   Dad is a good mechanic. [F]
      (iii)   Dad used to be a good mechanic. [F]
   b (i)   The car hasn't broken down. [F]
      (ii)   The family is now in St Tropez. [F]
   c (i)   Mr Beaton didn't buy a very good car. [T]
      (ii)   Mr Beaton bought a Rolls Royce. [F]
   d (i)   Steve thinks a mechanic will come if he phones the garage. [T]

3   *Answers:*
   a Type 1 *if + present tense + will + infinitive*
      Example: **d** If I phone the local garage they'll send a mechanic to fix the car.
      Function: D – a probable condition.
   b Type 2 *if + simple past + would + infinitive*
      Example: **a** The car wouldn't break down so often if Dad was a better mechanic.
      Function: A – an unlikely or unreal condition (present or future time).
   c Type 3 *if + past perfect + would + perfect infinitive*
      Example: **c** If I'd bought a better car we wouldn't have broken down.
      Function: B – an unreal condition in the past.
   d Mixed *if + past perfect + would + infinitive*
      Example: **b** If we hadn't broken down we would be in St Tropez by now.
      Function: C – unreal condition in past with unreal result in present.

Note: You may wish to point out the optional use of *were* rather than *was* in the 'if clause' of Type 2 conditional. Both are acceptable in present-day usage.

B   PRACTICE

Allow seven or eight minutes for each exercise.

4   *Answers:*
   a will miss   **b** was/were   **c** took
   d drive   **e** will leave   **f** lived
   g doesn't practise **h** would spend

5   *Answers:*
   a If Peter had brought a map he wouldn't be lost.
   b If I hadn't forgotten to bring my wallet I wouldn't be embarrassed.
   c If Sam hadn't missed the bus he wouldn't have been late.
   d If Juan hadn't fallen off his motorbike he wouldn't be in hospital.
   e If Lady Diana hadn't married Prince Charles she wouldn't have become famous.
   f If Emma had paid her tax bill she wouldn't have gone to prison.

C   COMMUNICATION

Allow five minutes for exercise 6 and ten minutes for exercise 7.

6   Divide the class into pairs to complete the sentence and to complete the matching exercise.

   If Thomas Edison hadn't been born, we wouldn't have electricity.
   Answers:
   1 C   2 E   3 A   4 D   5 B

7   Read through the sequence with the class. Ask each student to read a line each to illustrate how the chain works. Large classes should be divided into groups of about ten. The game will work better if students stand up in circles, and any student who makes a mistake has to sit down. The next student in the circle has to carry on where he/she left off. Keep the game going for six or seven minutes.

D   TEST

Allow ten minutes.

8   *Answers:*
   a would be
   f play
   b will find
   g had
   c had known
   h had made
   d win
   i would be
   e had brought
   j had remembered

FURTHER PRACTICE

AGE   Ex 68
GP   Ex 69.7

Holiday experiences

Verbs followed by infinitive or –ing

LESSON PLAN

Aim: To study and practise the use of:

(1) verbs which are followed by the infinitive (*decide, attempt, learn, choose, agree*);

(2) verbs which are followed by the –*ing* form (*feel like, suggest, enjoy, avoid, dislike*);

(3) verbs which are followed by either the infinitive or –*ing* form depending on their meaning (*stop, remember, forget, try*).

Topics: Holidays, friendship.

Lesson phases: Analysis and feedback 15 mins. Practice 15 mins. Communication 15 mins. Test 10 mins. Total 55 mins.

A ANALYSIS

Allow seven or eight minutes for each exercise.

1 *Answers:*

VERBS FOLLOWED BY:		
A *infinitive*	B *-ing*	C *infinitive or –ing depending on meaning*
decide agree attempt learn choose	feel like suggest enjoy avoid dislike	stop remember forget try

2 *Answers:*

	-ing	*infinitive*
a *stop*		
• to stop an action	✓	
• to stop in order to do something else		✓
b *remember*		
• recall something from the past	✓	
• remember to do something you might easily forget		✓
c *forget*		
• look back at something you didn't do in the past	✓	
• think about something you did in the past although you can't remember it		✓
d *try*		
• make an effort to do something difficult		✓
• do something as an experiment or test	✓	

B PRACTICE

Allow six or seven minutes for each exercise.

3 *Answers:*
  a Most people enjoy watching television.
  b I really must learn to drive soon.
  c Last year we decided to go to Florida.
  d My father agreed to pay for my new guitar.
  e I don't feel like going out this evening.
  f Clare dislikes living with her parents.
  g Sam suggested putting the money in a bank.
  h I try to avoid arguing with my girlfriend.

4 *Answers:*
  a to pack **b** to do **c** to put **d** packing **e** going
  f having **g** eating **h** eating **i** to give **j** to go

C COMMUNICATION

Allow fifteen minutes for this section.

5 Read through the advertisement with the class. Divide the students into pairs and ask each student to complete the questionnaire for his/her partner (by asking questions and writing in the answers). After ten minutes, re-group the students into groups of six or eight, checking that previous partners are not in the same group. Now ask the groups to compare the questionnaires and try to find suitable friends for their 'clients'.

It can be fun to get the groups to announce their suggestions to the whole class at the end of the exercise.

D TEST

Allow a maximum of ten minutes for the test.

6 *Answers:*

a (ii)	**b** (ii)	**c** (ii)	**d** (i)	**e** (i)
f (i)	**g** (ii)	**h** (ii)	**i** (i)	**j** (ii)

FURTHER PRACTICE

EGU Exs 53.1, 54.1, 56.1, 57.1

Eyewitness!

Verbs of perception with the present participle/infinitive

LESSON PLAN

Aim: To practise the use of the present participle and infinitive after verbs of perception and to make the students aware of the difference between the two.

Topics: Accidents and disasters.

Lesson phases: Analysis and feedback 25 mins. Practice 10 mins. Communication 15 mins. Test 5 mins. Total 55 mins.

A ANALYSIS

This section concentrates on the verbs of perception and illustrates to the students the difference between the use of the present participle and the infinitive after these verbs, i.e. the infinitive is used when the entire action is experienced, therefore more readily for short, complete actions; and the present participle is used either when the subject experiences only part of the action or when the action is of a continuous nature. This distinction is one which is easily blurred, even by native speakers, but which can sound odd if wrongly used. This section should take twenty to twenty-five minutes, allowing time for feedback and discussion.

1 This is just a simple sentence completion exercise to focus the students' attention on the passage.

   Answers:
   a ... having a walk by the port
   b ... the ground shake
   c ... the volcano roar   ... a column of flame shoot out
   d ... ran home   ... a few things   ... ran to the port
   e ... the boiling lava approaching
   f ... the lava flowing   ... it crushing houses

2 *Answers:*
   What do the verbs have in common? They are all verbs of perception/the senses.

Note At this point you could ask the students if they can think of any other verbs of perception, e.g. *notice, observe.*

   feel + (1) shake   (2) approaching
   hear + (1) roar   (2) shouting
   watch + flowing   smell + approaching
   see + shoot out
   listen to + crushing

3 This exercise first illustrates the distinction between the participle and the infinitive and then illustrates how they are used after verbs of perception.

   Answers:

	–ing form	infinitive
a We felt the ground shake.		✓
b We heard the volcano roar.		✓
c We saw a column of flame shoot out.		✓
d We could hear people shouting.	✓	
e We could smell and feel the lava approaching.	✓	
f We watched the lava flowing.	✓	
g We listened to the lava crushing the few houses in its path.	✓	

Draw time lines for other examples here if necessary. The students should answer that the infinitive of the second verb is used when the whole of the action is experienced (often a very short action).

If your students are having difficulty distinguishing between the two meanings, give the following sentences as examples of the distinction:

I heard the girl scream as she fell from the window.
We had to listen to the girls screaming through the whole concert.
We saw the vase fall to the floor and shatter.
We watched the potter making a new vase.

B PRACTICE

This section should only take about ten minutes.

4 *Answers:*
   a practising   **b** doing   **c** shatter   **d** playing
   e fall over   **f** cooking   **g** drop   **h** hit

For students who are still having problems you can explain that **c**, **e**, **g** and **h** are all very quick actions and one can't help but sense the whole action.

5 *Answers:*
   a explode/blow up   **b** shatter/break
   c jump   **d** break   **e** burning
   f gathering/standing/collecting
   g making/giving   **h** talking

C COMMUNICATION

This section should only take about fifteen minutes.

6 This exercise is a simple dialogue in pairs. Follow this procedure:
   - Focus the students' attention on the film poster and elicit from them what kind of film it is and what they might see in it.
   - Divide the students into pairs, A and B. Ask As to think of the questions they might ask B, based on the poster. Ask Bs to make notes about the film and what they experienced.
   - Give the students a few minutes to talk about the film. Swap roles if there is time. Monitor all the time for correct use of forms.
   - If you have some time to spare, widen the discussion out to discuss any experiences the students have had, using the verbs of perception.

D TEST

Allow about five minutes for doing and marking the test. Give two marks for each sentence (one per gap), making a total score out of ten.

7 *Answers:*
   a heard, crack   **b** smell, burning   **c** feel, tingling
   d see, hit   **e** listen to, practising

FURTHER PRACTICE

AGE   Ex 82
BEG   Ex 98

Christmas presents
Verbs with two objects

LESSON PLAN

Aims: To practise the use of verbs which take two objects, with special attention to the syntactical rules in the active and passive voice.

Topics: Giving presents, Christmas.

Lesson phases: Analysis and feedback 15 mins. Practice 15 mins. Communication 10 mins. Test 10 mins. Total 50 mins.

A ANALYSIS

Allow about five minutes for each exercise.

1 *Answers:*
   a Aunt Elizabeth gave Steven a bicycle.   Pattern **B**
   b Uncle Bill gave a watch to Teresa.   Pattern **A**
   c Steven gave Aunt Sarah a box of   Pattern **B**
   chocolates.
   d Harry gave perfume to Sylvia.   Pattern **A**
   The indirect object usually refers to a person.

2 *Answers:*
   a A bicycle was given to Steven by Aunt Elizabeth.
   b Teresa was given a watch by Uncle Bill.
   c A box of chocolates was given to Aunt Sarah by Steven.
   d Perfume was given to Sylvia by Harry.

   Explain to the students that the verbs can follow two patterns in the passive voice. You may wish to put this chart on the board to explain the rules:

   active
   Aunt Elizabeth gave Steven a bicycle.
   subject + verb + indirect object + direct object

   Uncle Bill gave a watch to Teresa.
   subject + verb + direct object + preposition + indirect object

   passive (using the same terminology as above)
   A bicycle was given to Steven by Aunt Elizabeth.
   direct object + verb + preposition + indirect object + by + subject

   Teresa was given a watch by Uncle Bill.
   indirect object + verb + direct object + by + subject

3 *Answers:*
   The verbs: *explained, described, suggested*
   The pattern they follow: ***subject + verb + direct object + to + indirect object***

B PRACTICE

Allow six or seven minutes for each exercise.

4 *Answers:*
   a Steven was given a bicycle by Aunt Elizabeth.
   b Harry bought Sylvia some perfume.
   c Steven gave Aunt Sarah a box of chocolates.
   d A watch was given to Teresa by Uncle Bill.
   e Steven bought a box of chocolates for Aunt Sarah.
   f Sylvia was sent some perfume by Harry.

5 *Answers:*
   a I was offered a cup of tea by Mrs Jackson.
   b My grandfather left me this house.
      My grandfather left this house to me.
   c The postman has brought you a parcel.
      The postman has brought a parcel for you.
   d She was paid fifty dollars by the manager.
   e Tom explained the operating instructions to me.
   f The architect has described the house designs to me.

C COMMUNICATION

Students should be able to complete this exercise in ten minutes.

6 Read through the instructions and divide the students into pairs to solve the problem.

   Suggested answers:
   Uncle Stephen sent a Turkish carpet for Mrs Armstrong.
   Aunt Mary sent an attaché case for Mr Armstrong.
   Uncle Henry sent an evening dress for Amanda.
   Aunt Mimi sent a dictionary for Carol.
   Aunt Harriet sent a calculator for Mike.
   Uncle Clive sent a watch for Philip.

D TEST

Allow ten minutes for completion of the test and checking.

7 *Answers:*
   a Hilary described her new dress to me.
   b No mistake.
   c My daughter was taken to the hospital by the ambulance.
   d The Highway Code was explained to me by my driving instructor.
   e No mistake.
   f A 10% bonus was given to Michael by his boss.
   g Patrick described the new design to Helen.
   h No mistake.
   i The guide suggested the Ritz Hotel to the rich tourists.
   j No mistake.

FURTHER PRACTICE

AGE   Ex 4

Partners

Stative and dynamic verbs

LESSON PLAN

Aim: To distinguish between stative and dynamic verbs and to practise their use with particular attention to the use of those verbs not normally used in the continuous tenses (stative verbs).

Topics: Relationships (boyfriends/girlfriends). Vocabulary relating to the senses, opinions and emotions, possession and mental state.

Lesson phases: Analysis and feedback 10 mins. Practice 15 mins. Communication 20 mins. Test 5 mins. Total 50 mins.

A ANALYSIS

Allow ten minutes for students to complete exercises 1 to 3. Exercise 3 can be done in pairs.

1 and 2 *Answers:*

A Verbs of possession

own	[✓]
belong to	[✓]
have (possession)	[✓]

B Verbs describing state of mind

know	[✓]
understand	[✓]
believe	[✓]
think (mental activity)	[ ]

C Verbs of opinion and emotion

love	[✓]
hate	[✓]
like	[✓]
dislike	[✓]
prefer	[✓]
think (have an opinion)	[✓]
feel (have an opinion)	[✓]
feel (describing emotion)	[ ]
wish	[✓]

D Verbs of the senses

see	[✓]
hear	[✓]
smell (state)	[✓]
smell (action)	[ ]
taste (state)	[✓]
taste (action)	[ ]
feel (state)	[✓]
feel (action)	[ ]

3 Elicit that when we are describing a state (i.e. an inherent quality which something possesses), we use simple tenses, and we use the continuous form to indicate an action. Contrast:

John is smelling the milk.
The milk smells fresh.
(John is *doing* something.)
(The milk itself *is* fresh.)

B PRACTICE

Allow a maximum of fifteen minutes for these two exercises.

4 *Answers:*
  a This pudding tastes delicious.
  b Some students think that English is difficult.
  c Those dirty socks smell disgusting!
  d Patrizio is thinking about his girlfriend.
  e The cook is tasting his new garlic sauce.
  f Many people believe in God.
  g The boutique owners are smelling the new perfume.
  h Carmen is feeling unhappy.
  i This old bed feels uncomfortable.
  j People who get up early hear the birds singing.

5 *Answers:*
  a tastes **b** belongs to **c** is smelling **d** love
  e am thinking **f** knows **g** is tasting **h** smells
  i feels **j** understand

C COMMUNICATION

6 Encourage the students to use their imagination – they can make their clients as ridiculous as they like. Allow five minutes for completion of the client record cards and then ten to fifteen minutes for the activity.

Allow students to stand up and move around the classroom. Encourage them to use the verbs of opinion and emotion in their questions and answers about their clients (i.e. *likes, loves, hates, dislikes, thinks, feels, wishes, prefers*). Leave time for a brief report-back phase in which students can report on their success (or lack of!) in finding suitable partners for their clients.

D TEST

Allow five minutes.

7 *Answers:*
  a is thinking **b** hates **c** dislikes **d** smelling
  e prefers **f** has **g** belongs to **h** knows **i** believes
  j doesn't know

FURTHER PRACTICE

No further practice for this unit.

18

Look it up!
Phrasal verbs

LESSON PLAN

Aims: To study and practise the use of some common phrasal verbs with particular attention to the position of noun and pronoun objects.

Topic: No overall topic area.

Lesson phases: Analysis and feedback 15 mins. Practice 15 mins. Game 10 mins. Test 10 mins. Total 50 mins.

A ANALYSIS

Allow ten minutes for exercise 1 and five minutes for exercise 2.

1 *Answers:*

a Mark visited Jimmy this morning.	[F]
b Jimmy will stop the disco if the neighbours complain.	[F]
c The party will be starting later than originally planned.	[T]
d There won't be any food at the party.	[F]
e Mark hopes that the girl will agree to come to the party.	[T]
1 to reduce sound	*turn down*
2 to refuse an invitation	*turn down*
3 to bring something to a particular place	*bring over*
4 to telephone someone	*call up*
5 to change something to a later time	*put back*
6 to organise/arrange something	*set up*
7 to find information in a book	*look up*

2 Check that the students understand the meaning of 'particle', 'pronoun' and 'noun object'. Point out that all phrasal verbs are made up of a main noun and particle. Put this diagram on the board if necessary:

verb	**particle**	
↓	↓	
ring	*up*	
verb	**noun object**	**particle**
↓	↓	↓
ring	*Jimmy*	*up*
verb	**pronoun**	**particle**
↓	↓	↓
ring	*him*	*up*

Answers:

verb + pronoun + particle
  rang him up
  turn me down

verb + particle + pronoun
verb + noun object + particle
  turn the volume down
  bringing the food over

verb + particle + noun object
  set up a disco
  looked up the number

a ***verb + particle + pronoun*** is not possible with phrasal verbs.

b The example of a phrasal verb in the passive form is: *The party has been put back.*
The pattern is: ***object + passive verb + particle***

B PRACTICE

Allow six or seven minutes for each exercise.

3 Note: The following verbs are introduced for the first time here:
put up, put forward (with meaning of 'to suggest'), *bring back.*

Answers:
a Why don't you look it up in the dictionary?
b Hilary will ring her up this afternoon.
c That radio's too loud, please turn it down.
d Can you put it back?
e Ali is setting it up in the lobby.
f We put it up in a field.
g Why don't you put it forward (to the committee)?
h Don't forget to bring them back tomorrow.

4 *Answers:*
a put, up   **b** brought, on   **c** up, set   **d** turned, up
e turn, off

C GAME

It should take about ten minutes for students to complete the game.

5 Ask students to work in pairs.

Answers:

put out	*extinguish*
call off	*cancel*
bring over	*deliver*
ring up	*phone*
bring back	*return*
put off	*delay*
take on	*employ*
take up	*start*
put forward	*suggest*
blow up	*explode*
turn down	*refuse*

```
C A N C E L L V T D
R S G E X P L O D E
E B I O T U P W E L
T D E L I V E R M A
U C M X N Y E S P Y
R S U G G E S T L Q
N P X M U V A A O Z
C R D P I O N R Y M
R E F U S E L T W Q
J D W P H O N E A Z
```

D TEST

Allow ten minutes for the test and checking of answers.

6 *Answers:*
a blew it up
b turn it down
c rang them up
d put it off
e look it up
f brought it back
g turned it down
h brought them over
i put it out
j called it off

FURTHER PRACTICE

EGU	Exs 130.2, 130.2
GP	Exs 45.1–45.7

English is spoken here

Passives

LESSON PLAN

Aim: To practise the use of the following tenses in the passive voice: present simple, present perfect, past simple, future simple (see below). Also to practise the use of modal verbs in the passive voice e.g. *must, can, should, will* (as in future simple).

Topic: Labels and notices, general knowledge.

Lesson phases: Analysis and feedback 15 mins. Practice 15 mins. Game 10 mins. Test 10 mins. Total 50 mins.

A ANALYSIS

Allow three or four minutes for each exercise.

1 **a** Discuss these suggested answers with students:
   A Television programme credits
   B In a shop window
   C On a shirt label
   D On a railway notice board
   E In a theatre programme
   F On a packet of fruit juice

   b Elicit that **D** is different because the 'agent' is mentioned. If students are unfamiliar with this, explain that the agent is the cause of the action described by the verb – in an active sentence it would be the subject of the verb.

2 Check that the students understand the reasons and discuss which reasons apply to the notices in exercise 1 (there is no fixed answer).

3 Elicit some of the reasons given in exercise 2 to explain why the sentences would be better in the passive form – point out that it is not necessary to include the agent.

   Answers:
   a We apologise that flight KL167 has been cancelled because of weather conditions.
   b Refunds can be obtained from the ticket office.
   c Drinks will be served in the hotel lounge at six o'clock.
   d Payment by Eurocheque is accepted in this shop.
   e This movie was filmed on location in Ireland.

	active	*passive*
present simple	accept speaks	is accepted is spoken
past simple	filmed recorded	was filmed was recorded
present perfect	has cancelled have delayed	has been cancelled have been delayed
modal verbs	must wash can obtain will serve must not dry clean should refrigerate	must be washed can be obtained will be served must not be dry cleaned should be refrigerated

B PRACTICE

Allow five minutes for each exercise.

4 Point out that the students will need to put the verbs into the correct tense to fit the sentence context.

Answers:
a The bank was robbed last night.
b Travellers cheques are accepted in this store.
c This pullover should be washed by hand.
d Your new car will be delivered tomorrow.
e The first prize was won by a man from Manchester.
f Penicillin was discovered by Alexander Fleming.
g Britain has not been invaded since the year 1066.
h This account must be paid within 28 days.
i The hotel rooms are cleaned every day.
j Next week your class will be taught by Mrs Girton.

5 *Answers:*
a This hotel serves breakfast between 8 and 10 a.m.
b Scientists have discovered a cure for cancer at last!
c The zoo keepers will feed the monkeys at four o'clock.
d The engineer installed the computer two months ago.
e You can wash this shirt at any temperature.

C GAME

Allow ten minutes for completion of the game.

6 The Sentence Jigsaw
Explain the task. Divide the class into groups of three: A, B and C in each group (students may double up role A if numbers do not fit exactly). Check that students only look at their own sections and communicate through speech only.

Answers:

America	was discovered by	Christopher Columbus
Radio	was invented by	Marconi
Mercedes cars	are manufactured	in Germany
Coffee	is exported	from Colombia
Crimes	are investigated	by detectives
Islands	are surrounded	by water
Chinese food	should be eaten	with chopsticks
President Kennedy	was assassinated	in Dallas
The 1812 Overture	was composed	by Tchaikovsky
Guernica	was painted	by Pablo Picasso
Japan	is ruled	by an Emperor
Most buildings	are designed	by architects
War and Peace	was written	by Leo Tolstoy

D TEST

Allow ten minutes for completion of the test and checking.

7 *Answers:*
a Photographs may be taken in this museum.
b The keys have been lost.
c Many famous crimes were investigated by Sherlock Holmes.
d A cure for the common cold has been discovered!
e Your letters will be sent on to your new address.
f The sheets are changed every week.
g A lot of hamburgers are eaten in the United States.
h Dogs must not be brought into this park.
i The best outfits this season have been designed by the Italians.
j This TV was manufactured in Korea.

FURTHER PRACTICE

AGE	Ex 10
BEG	Ex 66
EGU	Exs 42.1, 42.3, 43.1, 43.2
GP	19.1, 19.2, 19.5–19.7

Hand of death

-ed and -ing adjectives

LESSON PLAN

Aims: To distinguish between present and past participles used as adjectives (i.e. adjectives ending -ing and -ed) and to practise their use.

Topics: Horror films, advertising, Bath.

Lesson phases: Analysis and feedback 15 mins. Practice 15 mins. Communication 10 mins. Test 10 mins. Total 50 mins.

A ANALYSIS

Allow five minutes for each exercise.

1 Elicit descriptions/reactions to the poster as a warm up.

The two words which describe how the critics felt: *shocked, horrified.*
The two words which describe the film: *terrifying, revolting.*

2 *Answers:*

	own feelings	describing film
a ... boring ...		✓
b ... thrilling ...		✓✓
c ... horrified ...	✓	
d ... petrified ...	✓	
e ... disgusting ...		✓
f ... shocked ...	✓	

3 *Answers:*

	actor	friend
a He was really terrifying.	✓	
b She was totally bored.		✓
c He was absolutely disgusting.	✓	
d She was electrifying.	✓	

The general rule which can be deduced from the examples:
-ed: used to describe the way a person feels.
-ing: used to describe the thing or person which causes us to have a reaction.
e.g. I felt *terrified* because the film was *terrifying.*

B PRACTICE

Allow five or six minutes for each exercise and two or three minutes for checking.

4 *Answers:*
a Edwin is a charming host; he makes all his guests feel *relaxed.*
b I thought that meal was *disgusting* – it tasted revolting!
c Small children can be very infuriating; they often make me feel *annoyed.*
d I am usually confused by cricket; it is certainly *complicated*!
e Don't expect to be *excited* by that play; I thought it was very disappointing.

5 *Answers:*
a embarrassed b interesting, bored c amazing
d depressed e confusing f exhausting, tired
g exciting, fascinating h exhilarating, terrified

C COMMUNICATION

6 Go through the example with the class and explain any vocabulary problems with the other posters. Divide the class into groups of three or four. Allow ten minutes, perhaps a little longer if students find the tasks stimulating. The second task may be omitted with weaker classes or if time is limited.

Weaker or less imaginative students may need some help. Here are some suggested slogans:

Is your social life boring? Make life exciting with Star Social Club.
Are your meals boring? Your dinner guests will be amazed at your cooking if you buy our New Cookery Course!
Are you embarrased by your teeth? They will be dazzling if you use new Sparklo-dent!

D TEST

Allow ten minutes for completion of the exercise and checking.

7 *Answers:*
a invigorating b tired c relaxing d bored
e exciting f disgusting g appalling h interested
i charming j fascinating

FURTHER PRACTICE

BEG   Ex 100
EGUY   Exs 94.1–94.3
PG3   Unit 2, Ex 9

Describing objects

Order of adjectives before a noun

LESSON PLAN

Aim: To make students aware that there is an order of adjectives before nouns and to give them the strategies to be able to work out the order when faced with a number of adjectives.

Topic: Describing nouns.

Lesson phases: Analysis and feedback 25 mins. Practice 10 mins. Communication 20 mins. Test 5 mins. Total 60 mins.

A   ANALYSIS

Allow about fifteen minutes for the students to do the exercises here and ten minutes for checking. There should be no real problems in understanding but some of the groupings of the adjectives may need explanation, and exercise 3 requires some logical thought.

1   *Answers:*   **a** 4   **b** 6   **c** 1   **d** 3   **e** 5   **f** 2

2   *Answers:*
a   **a** delightful   **b** amazing   **e** beautiful   **f** disgusting
b   Sentence **b**. The number comes first.
c   Sentences **c, d, e**
    Defining words – sports, terraced, wedding
d   *Age:* nineteenth-century, new, two-year-old, modern, antique, old

Note: Point out here that 'age' is a general term and that expressions such as *old-fashioned, up-to-date* etc. are included.
Colour: bright red, brown
Note: Point out here that any adjectives which qualify the colour always precede it directly e.g. *bright.*
Defining adjective/noun: sports, terraced, wedding
Material: wooden, pearl, brick-built, gold
Nationality: Russian, Italian
Opinion: delightful, amazing, beautiful, disgusting
Size: tiny, little
The one adjective that does not fit in these categories is *expensive.* For the purposes of this unit, this one has been categorised as general.

3   *Answers:*
a   T
b   F Age comes before colour (sentences C and F)
c   T
d   T
e   F Material comes after nationality (sentence B)
f   F Nationality comes after colour (sentence C)
g   F Opinion comes before size (sentence A)

The True/False exercise helps to prepare the students for this next section, which is quite difficult. If they find it too difficult, provide the order for them.

Order of adjectives: **number**, *opinion*, **general**, *size, age,* **colour**, *nationality, material, defining adjective/noun,* **noun**.

Note: It is worth pointing out that we rarely use more than two or three adjectives before the noun, even in writing. If the students try to remember opinion, size, age, colour, nationality, they should be able to order most adjectives.

B   PRACTICE

Allow about ten minutes for the exercises and checking this section. The students should not have any difficulties.

4   *Answers:*
a   two lovely, comfortable, *black* leather chairs.
b   most incredible up-to-date *Japanese* computer.
c   a really elegant, *huge*, white-and-grey office.
d   six lovely crystal *wine* glasses.
e   a *beautiful*, very tall, red-headed woman. (OR very *beautiful*, tall …)
f   a very nice, *small*, English class.
g   *several* very expensive Italian silk shirts.
h   a pair of *antique* silver earrings.

5   *Answers:*
Encourage the students to put the indefinite article before the adjectives here, to make more acceptable phrases.
a   a cheap, old, Polish car
b   an attractive, modern, black plastic hi-fi system
c   a modern, Swedish, smoked glass dining table
d   a good-looking, tall, Scottish policeman (OR tall, good-looking …)
e   a hard, black, fibre-glass riding hat
f   a short, yellow, lead pencil
g   a burgundy, ceramic table lamp
h   a small, brown-and-white French poodle

C   COMMUNICATION

6   Allow about ten minutes for this exercise and encourage the students to use a variety of adjectives. Follow this procedure:

● Each student thinks of the adjectives.
● They write a sentence about each picture. Monitor for correct order of adjectives in the sentences.
● In pairs, they combine their adjectives to make one sentence about each picture.
● Ask some of the students to read their sentences out.

Note: As the guidelines given here are very general, you may find that some of the adjectives the students suggest may not easily fit the criteria given. If so, fit them in the sentences according to the general-specific rule and where they sound most natural.

D   TEST

Allow only about five minutes for the students to do the test. Give two marks for each group of adjectives correctly formed, making a score out of ten.
Note: Tell your students that *Persian* is a type of cat.

7   *Answers:*
a   a really interesting science-fiction book about a huge, twenty-first century, American space station.
b   a tiny, six-week-old, grey Persian kitten.
c   a long, red, leather coat.
d   three expensive French perfumes

General note: Alert your students to the punctuation used with adjectives: they are separated with commas only according to ease of pronunciation and meaning within the sentence, for example, in exercise 1, sentence **e** *antique* and *gold* are separated by a comma to show that the ring is an *antique*, otherwise antique could refer to the type of gold.

FURTHER PRACTICE   EGU   Ex 95.1

References

Position of adverbs

LESSON PLAN

Aim: To examine and practise the use of mid-position adverbs with particular attention to the position relative to main, auxiliary and modal verbs.

Topics: Job references, famous people.

Lesson phases: Analysis and feedback 15 mins. Practice 10 mins. Game 15 mins. Test 10 mins. Total 50 mins.

A ANALYSIS

Allow six or seven minutes for each exercise plus two minutes for checking.

1 Read through the introduction and explain the purpose of job references if students are unfamiliar with these. Students should discuss question **a** and reach their own conclusion.

*Question **b** answers:*
Stephen Briggs' letter:
always, usually, really, often, badly, rarely, really, sincerely.

Joanna Goldsmith's letter:
currently, already, never, sometimes, well, hardly, occasionally, definitely, sincerely.

2 *Answers:*
 a Where do most adverbs go in sentences?
 before the verb.
 Example: He really enjoys administrative work.
 b What happens when there is more than one part to the verb, for example *has been promoted* or *doesn't get involved*?
 The adverb goes after the first auxiliary verb.
 Example: (He) has always been punctual.
 She has already been promoted twice.
 c What happens when there is a modal verb, for example *can recommend*?
 The adverb goes between the modal verb and the main verb.
 Example: I can definitely recommend her.
 d What happens when the verb is *am, are, is* or *were*?
 The adverb goes after am, are, is and were.
 Example: He is usually the first person to arrive.
 • *Which two adverbs* always go after the main verb?
 well, badly.
 Example: He works badly when under pressure.

B PRACTICE

Allow five minutes for each exercise.

3 *Answers:*
 a She's never been to New York.
 b I can easily answer that question.
 c He is occasionally late because of the traffic.
 d I eat well when I go to my mother's house.
 e Percy doesn't really like spicy food.
 f Tourists should always carry their passports with them.
 g I have recently started learning Arabic.
 h Children behave badly when they are tired.

4 *Answers:*
 a Amsterdam is usually known as the Venice of the North.
 b My parents have never been abroad in their lives.
 c You should never have taken such foolish advice.
 d I always sleep well after a hard day's work.
 e That poor child has hardly ever eaten a proper meal.

C GAME

Allow the game to continue for about fifteen minutes.

5 Read through the instructions and the example with the class. If necessary, point out that the person in question here is Queen Elizabeth. Divide the students into large groups. (This can be a whole class activity if the class is small.) Check that everyone has completed their five sentences before starting the game – some less imaginative students may need help with suggestions of famous people. Here are some ideas you might give them:
Napoleon Bonaparte
Christopher Columbus
Princess Diana
Marilyn Monroe
Julius Caesar
President Kennedy
Mikhail Gorbachev
Michael Jackson
Paul McCartney
Mike Tyson

D TEST

Allow ten minutes for the test.

6 *Answers:*
 a I usually sleep badly when I am worried about something.
 b No mistake.
 c Henry's team has easily beaten all the others.
 d Sophia is rarely late for her lessons.
 e Is Emma definitely coming to the theatre with us?
 f My family has always lived on a farm.
 g Soldiers usually obey their officers.
 h No mistake.
 i Children should always listen to their parents.
 j In historic times most people were frequently ill.

FURTHER PRACTICE

EGU   Exs 106.1, 106.2

All in the home
Prepositions of location

LESSON PLAN

Aim: To illustrate the differences between prepositions of location and to practise them.

Topics: Places and furniture in the home; safety in the home.

Lesson phases: Analysis and feedback 15 mins. Practice 10 mins. Communication 15 mins. Test 10 mins. Total 50 mins.

A ANALYSIS

This section illustrates prepositions of location by pictures. The students should not have any problems here, except perhaps the difference between *in front of* and *opposite*. Make sure that the students understand that *opposite* contains the idea of 'facing', whereas *in front of* does not.

1 *Answers:*
   a 3 **b** 4 **c** 5 **d** 6 **e** 1 **f** 2 **g** 7 **h** 9 **i** 8 **j** 10

2 *Answers:*
   a at **b** under **c** next to **d** behind **e** in
   f on **g** in front of **h** near **i** by **j** opposite

B PRACTICE

The first exercise is a straightforward gap fill, but the second, as well as being a gap fill, can act as a communicative exercise for students if there is time, to extend use of the prepositions a little. If the exercise is not extended, these two should take no more than ten minutes.

3 *Answers:*
   a at **b** in **c** next to/near **d** on **e** under
   f opposite **g** behind **h** by

4 *Answers:*
   DO
   – put a guard in front of an open fire
   – keep tools and other sharp objects in a cupboard
   – keep medicines behind closed doors
   – encourage your children to keep their toys in a toy box
   – keep a fire extinguisher by/near the cooker

   DON'T
   – put vases of flowers on the television
   – hang clothes in front of a fire or an electric heater
   – run electrical wires under a carpet
   – stand on chairs or stools
   – leave sharp knives on the work surfaces in the kitchen

If your students have time, encourage them to make up some tips of their own, using prepositions.

C COMMUNICATION

This section should only take about fifteen minutes.

5 This exercise is a 'find the difference' exercise between two very similar drawings. However, the students also have to try to ascertain the occupation of the owner of the room. Follow this procedure:

   • Divide the students into pairs and make sure they know which picture each one is looking at.
   • Tell them they each have to find nine hidden objects in their pictures, and to make a note individually of what the objects are and where they are hidden.
   • The students now work in pairs and find the differences between their pictures, in terms of where the objects are hidden. Monitor for correct use of prepositions, and make sure the students are not looking at each other's pictures.
   • The students can then check by looking at the other picture.
   • Ask the students what the room owner's profession is. The hidden objects give the impression that he/she may be a spy.

   Objects: knife, gun, passport, money, secret documents, tickets, camera, dictionary, alarm clock.

D TEST

Give two marks for each correct sentence, making a total of ten.

6 *Answers:*
   a Where shall I put this vase?
       Put it on the table in the lounge.
   b Let me take your photo here; stand in front of the fountain and behind that lovely bush. (or in front of that bush and . . .)
   c Where shall I wait for you?
       Wait on the bench by the river.
   d Can these animals be put together?
       You can put the cat next to the dog but not near the fish.
   e Where is the complaints desk?
       It's at the main entrance under the stairs.

FURTHER PRACTICE

AGE   Ex 169
EGU   Exs 117.1–117.3
GP   Exs 66.2, 66.3

Michael Jackson

Prepositions of time

LESSON PLAN

Aim: To clarify in the students' minds when we use the prepositions of time (*at, by, during, for, from . . . till, in, on, since*) and the combinations with nouns in which they appear.

Topics: Famous people; details about people's lives.

Lesson phases: Analysis and feedback 20 mins. Practice 15 mins. Communication 15 mins. Test 5 mins. Total 55 mins.

A ANALYSIS

This section looks at prepositions of time, and which prepositions accompany which concepts, e.g. dates, times etc. The analysis is fairly simple and shouldn't take more than a few minutes.

1 *Answers:*

Born 29 August 1958
Turned professional age nine
First tour age eleven, 1969
First chart single age eleven
First film appearance 1975
Went solo 1978
Likes relaxing at home with pet chimpanzee

Most of the answers above can be either dates or ages.

2 Check that the students have underlined all the prepositions.

3 Not all of the answers here come from the passage, but allow students to use their own knowledge, and then to use the clues under the chart.

Answers (when exercise 3 is complete):

	at	by	during	for	from ... till	in	on	since
age	✓	✓			✓			✓
day		✓			✓		✓	✓
date		✓	✓		✓		✓	✓
year		✓	✓	✓	✓	✓		✓
period of time				✓				
time	✓	✓			✓		✓	✓
season		✓	✓		✓	✓		✓
festival	✓	✓			✓			✓

It might be necessary to give the students some help here.

4 *Answers:*
a point in time: *at, by, in, on, since*
a period of time duration: *during, for, from . . . till*

B PRACTICE

These two simple exercises should only take about ten to fifteen minutes.

5 *Answers:*
a on **b** in **c** on **d** in **e** at **f** at **g** at **h** during/in **i** at **j** in **k** at **l** at **m** for/in **n** at

6 *Answers:*
The wording here may vary, but check that the prepositions are correct.

1 I'm free at Christmas and would like to visit you. I can come on the 24th, at six o'clock, and I can stay till the 29th. Perhaps we could visit Gran during that period. Please phone me on Sunday. I'll be in from ten till eleven thirty.

2 Elena Lopez was born in 1973 and is now aged 18. She was thought to be in Columbia from 1987 to 1989, then was in China during the riots in 1989. Find her.

3 Lucy arrived in London in May and has been with me from June till now. She wants to go to Switzerland in the winter and would like to stay with you for three months, from November till February. I need to know by October.

C COMMUNICATION

This exercise is likely to take quite a long time because of the preparation. Make sure that your students know exactly what they have to do.

7 Follow this procedure:

- Ask the students to think of someone famous if they can, someone about whom they know quite a lot. If not, they can think of a friend, or use themselves.
- Tell them to write notes about this person, using prepositions to give a potted history of their life. It is therefore better if the notes are interesting, so encourage them to use their imagination.
- In pairs, the students then tell each other about their 'person', while their partners write the details down in a biodata form. They should swap forms to check that everything is correct. Monitor the use of prepositions throughout.

D TEST

Allow only five minutes for this test. Give scores out of ten.

8 *Answers:*
a in **b** on **c** at **d** in **e** from . . . till **f** in **g** since **h** during **i** at **j** on

FURTHER PRACTICE

BEG   Ex 142
EGU   Exs 114.1, 114.2
GP   Exs 65.1–65.4
PG3   Unit 4, Exs 1–2

An eventful day!

Prepositions and adverbs of time

LESSON PLAN

Aim: To clarify the use of the most common time prepositions and adverbs, (*after, as, before, during, for, since, until, when, while*), and distinguish the two.

Topics: Town facilities; accidents.

Lesson phases: Analysis and feedback 25 mins. Practice 10 mins. Communication 15 mins. Test 10 mins. Total 60 mins.

A   ANALYSIS

The letter in this section illustrates the uses of the time prepositions and adverbs practised here. The first exercise is basically comprehension, then the others analyse the uses. The students should find exercises 2 and 3 quite easy, and there should not be much need for teacher help.

1   *Answers:* (order followed by times in brackets)
   a 7 (13.00)   **b** 10 (approx 14.15–14.30)
   c 3 (approx 10.00)   **d** 12 (after 16.00)   **e** 6 (11.45)
   f 1 (9.00)   **g** 9 (14.00)   **h** 11 (15.30)   **i** 8 (13.15–13.30)
   j 5 (11.00)   **k** 4 (10.30)   **l** 2 (approx 9.30)

   The times are given in the letter in some cases, but in others they have to be worked out and are very approximate.

2   Check that the students have underlined the correct words.
   Answers:

after I left the supermarket four	*for* another half an hour ages
as I was leaving	*since* two
before he could see me about 2.30 pm	I left you last night
during the day	*until* two
	they'd found the right tickets
	when I arrived …
	while I was out

3   Check that the students do understand the difference between a clause and a noun.
   Answers:

	can be followed by	
	a clause	*a noun*
after	✓	✓
as	✓	
before	✓	✓
during		✓
for		✓
since	✓	✓
until	✓	✓
when	✓	
while	✓	

B   PRACTICE

This section is fairly simple and should only take about ten minutes.

4   Some phrases in this exercise can combine with more than one other. However, the answers given below can be arrived at by elimination if they are all to be sensible.
   Answers:
   a 4   **b** 7   **c** 1   **d** 9   **e** 3   **f** 10   **g** 5   **h** 2   **i** 8   **j** 6

5   *Answers:*
   a while   **b** for   **c** when   **d** since   **e** during   **f** before

C   COMMUNICATION

This exercise uses the story from the letter as a model for the students to practise the prepositions and adverbs in a freer way and to create a story themselves.

6   Follow this procedure:
   - Divide the students into pairs, A and B, and make sure they know which set of pictures to look at, and that they must not show their pictures to their partner.
   - Tell them to make notes about the pictures each person has got, which form half of a story. Remind them to use the prepositions and adverbs as they are making notes.
   - The students work in their pairs. Each student describes the story of each picture, using either 'I', or giving the girl a name.
   - In pairs the students piece the story together orally. Monitor for correct use of structure and especially for use of the time adverbs for linking.
   - Ask one or two of the better pairs to narrate their story to the class. The other students listen and correct if necessary.
   - The students could write the letter illustrated in frame H for homework.

D   TEST

Allow a few minutes for the students to do the test and then mark it in class. Give students marks out of ten.

7   *Answers:*
   a after   **b** since   **c** while/when*   **d** during/in**
   e for   **f** before   **g** until   **h** until   **i** as   **j** when/while*
   *both adverbs are acceptable.
   **in* is possible here, though not examined in this unit.

FURTHER PRACTICE

EGU   Exs 115.1–115.3

Can you count it?

Countable and uncountable nouns

LESSON PLAN

Aim: To distinguish between countable and uncountable nouns and to practise their use with articles, quantifiers and determiners.

Topic: No overall topic area.

Lesson phases: Analysis and feedback 15 mins. Practice 15 mins. Communication 10 mins. Test 10 mins. Total 50 mins.

A ANALYSIS

Allow five minutes for exercise 1 and ten minutes for exercise 2 including checking.

1 *Answers:*

countable	uncountable
agency	accommodation
flats	furniture
houses	health
chairs	happiness
sofas	music
club	travel
hobbies	research
parties	advice
investigations	countryside
hotels	scenery

2 *Answers:*

		countable	uncountable
They can be used with these words:	a/an	[✓]	[ ]
	the	[✓]	[✓]
	much	[ ]	[✓]
	many	[✓]	[ ]
	a lot of	[✓]	[✓]
	a few	[✓]	[ ]
They have a plural form		[✓]	[ ]
They take a singular verb		[ ]	[✓]

B PRACTICE

Allow six or seven minutes for each exercise.

3 *Answers:*
   a information **b** luggage **c** advice **d** Does
   e baggage **f** a lot of **g** equipment **h** It's **i** journey
   j permission

4 *Answers:*
   a My sister is very clever – she knows so many facts.
   b I'm doing research into Chinese history for my degree./ I'm doing some research ... etc
   c Antique English furniture is very expensive.
   d I like two spoonfuls of sugar with my coffee.
   e Mathematics is difficult for me.
   f My father gives me too much advice.
   g Travel? I hate it.
   h English has too many words and too much grammar!

C COMMUNICATION

Allow about ten minutes for this exercise.

5 Explain the instructions to the class and divide the students into pairs. Insist that students only look at their own information. When pairs have finished, elicit the answers and discuss the meaning of the quotations/ sayings with the class. The authors of the quotations are noted in brackets below.

   Answers:
   Sayings
   a You can't buy happiness.
   b There is no peace for the wicked.
   c Travel broadens the mind.
   d A little knowledge is a dangerous thing.

   Quotations
   e Advice is seldom welcome, and those who need it the most always like it the least. (Earl of Chesterfield)
   f Architecture is frozen music. (Friedrich Von Schelling)
   g I love work. I can sit and look at it for hours. (Jerome K. Jerome)
   h Punctuality is the politeness of kings. (Louis XVIII)

D TEST

Allow ten minutes for completion of the exercise and checking.

6 *Answers:*
   a is **b** scenery **c** much **d** was **e** a lot of
   f homework **g** much **h** some **i** much **j** is

FURTHER PRACTICE

AGE   Ex 141
EGU   Exs 69.1, 69.3
GP   Exs 48.2, 48.3, 48.5

This is the life!

The use of the definite article

LESSON PLAN

Aim: To clarify the use of the definite article in English, particularly in comparison with the non-use of the article.

Topics: Life in the country and the city.

Lesson phases: Analysis and feedback 25 mins. Practice 10 mins. Communication 15 mins. Test 10 mins. Total 60 mins.

A ANALYSIS

Allow about fifteen to twenty minutes for the students to work through the exercises in this section and a few more minutes for discussion and clarification.

1 *Answers:*

   a F **b** F **c** F **d** T **e** F **f** F

   The students could also correct the false statements.

2 This exercise concentrates on the distinction between nouns used in a general and specific way, and focuses the students' minds on the fact that the definite article is usually used with nouns with a specific meaning. This unit looks only at this very restricted use of the article. If students are unsure what is meant by general and specific, ask if the noun refers to only one, e.g. garden (a specific one), or gardens as a concept (general).

   Answers:

   a, c, i and **l** are general; all the others are specific.

   The difference between the nouns mentioned at the end of the exercise is that those with the article refer to one particular school and hospital, (i.e. the building) rather than the institution; and one type of fear, rather than abstract, general fear.

3 This exercise looks at the specific, or defined, use of nouns, and asks students to analyse how these nouns can be recognised as definite, for example, if defined by a relative clause or a following phrase which defines (e.g. a noun phrase such as *of wasps and bees*), by the fact that there is only one of these nouns in the context, or by a previous mention. It might be necessary to explain these ideas to the students before they attempt this exercise.

   Answers:

	relative clause	following phrase	only one	previous mention
the life I lived in London	✔			
the fear of wasps and bees		✔		
the village is lovely				✔
the garden is delightful			✔	
the street I live in	✔			
I'm used to the hospital			✔	
Sam's happy with the school			✔	
the shop where Mary works	✔			

B PRACTICE

These exercises should only take a few minutes if the students have understood the concept.

4 *Answers:*

   b, c, e and **h** require the article; the others do not.

5 *Answers:*

   a Man should try to live with nature.
   b I want to go to university after leaving school.
   c Where's Sam? I think he's in the garden.
   d The sun goes round the earth.
   e I prefer living in the city to living in the country.
   f The town where my brother lives is rather industrial.
   g Beauty is in the eye of the beholder.
   h The use of colour makes that painting.

C COMMUNICATION

This section is based on a fairly structural team game.

6 Make sure that the students know that this is a competition, and that you are the judge. It might be useful to have a dictionary or two at hand for this exercise. Follow this procedure:

   - Divide the class into two teams. If you have a large class, you might wish to make four teams, and either have them playing separately, or alter the game to have four teams playing.
   - Refer the teams to the boxes containing nouns on their sheets.
   - Ask Team A to choose a noun (e.g. *love*) and call it out. They then write a sentence containing the noun without the article, e.g. *Everyone likes being in love.* Team B writes a sentence containing the noun with the article, e.g. *The love of a mother for her child is very pure.*
     (To make this more interesting with a good class, each team member can write a sentence, and then the team decides together on the best one.)
   - After a set time limit, the two teams read out their sentences. Give up to five marks according to accuracy, use (or otherwise) of the article and naturalness of the sentence.
   - Team B chooses a noun, they write the sentence without the article, and so on. Go through about six nouns if time allows, then decide which team is the winner.

D TEST

Allow only about five minutes for the test and five for checking in the class. Give marks out of ten.

7 *Answers:*

   a, b, d and **g** require the article; the others do not.

FURTHER PRACTICE

No further practice for this unit.

A night at the movies

Question tags

LESSON PLAN

Aim: To study the construction of question tags when used to elicit confirmation, and to practise their use.

Topic: Cinema: films, film stars, plots etc.

Lesson phases: Analysis and feedback 10 mins. Practice 20 mins. Game 15 mins. Test 10 mins. Total 55 mins.

A   ANALYSIS

Allow five minutes for each exercise.

1 Check the following vocabulary: *plot, special effects, model, to be convincing.* You may wish to read the dialogue aloud. It is important to use a falling tune on each question tag:

e.g. We've seen him on TV, haven't we?

Answers:

a	Sue expects Chuck to agree that the plot was obvious.	[T]
b	Chuck thinks that the explosion looked realistic.	[F]
c	Chuck expects Sue to agree that the hero wasn't convincing.	[T]
d	Sue thinks that Chuck will probably want to eat something.	[T]

Point out that question tags with a falling tune usually mean that we expect the listener to agree or confirm what we have said. When we are not sure that the listener will agree or confirm, we use a rising tune. Question tags with a rising tune, although carrying a different attitude, are grammatically identical with those spoken with a falling tune.

2 *Answers:*

sentence verb	question tag
was	wasn't
didn't look	did
could see	couldn't
have seen	haven't

sentence subject	question tag
the plot	it
the hero	he
you	you
we	we

Point out that the question tag for 'let's' is 'shall we?'

B   PRACTICE

Allow five minutes for each exercise.

3 *Answers:*
   a 6   **b** 9   **c** 2   **d** 8   **e** 4   **f** 10   **g** 5   **h** 7   **i** 1   **j** 3

4 *Answers:*
   a weren't they?   **b** could she?   **c** has she?
   d didn't they?   **e** shouldn't we?   **f** shall we?

5 *Answers:*
   a wasn't   **b** Let's   **c** can   **d** is   **e** don't   **f** should

C   GAME

6 Allow ten to fifteen minutes for the game. Follow this procedure:

- It will help students to understand the game if you demonstrate with a student. Pick a student from the class and tell him/her that he/she must answer your questions immediately and honestly, but he/she mustn't say yes or no. Lead the student into a dialogue like this example:

Teacher	What's your name?
Student	Paolo.
Teacher	Did you say Paolo?
Student	That's correct.
Teacher	You're a student, aren't you?
Student	Yes, I ...
Teacher	Out!!

- Show the class that by repeating or rephrasing the same question, and by using question tags, they can usually trick the contestant into saying 'yes' or 'no'.
- Divide the class into groups of about six to play the game. They can take it in turns to be the questioner and/or the contestant. One person in each group should keep a record of how long each student is able to keep answering without saying 'yes' or 'no' in order to find the winner.

D   TEST

Allow ten minutes for this exercise.

7 *Answers:*
   a won't they?
   b isn't he?
   c was it?
   d can't they?
   e shall we?
   f has she?
   g do they?
   h doesn't he?
   i should we?
   j will you?

FURTHER PRACTICE

AGE	Ex 20
BEG	Exs 54, 55
EGU	Exs 52.1–52.3
GP	Exs 41.4, 41.5
PG3	Unit 13, Exs 3, 5

Anyone for tennis?

All, both, every, each, none, neither

LESSON PLAN

Aim: To clarify the differences between the above and to practise them.

Topic: Tennis; sports; sports clothes.

Lesson phases: Analysis and feedback 25 mins. Practice 10 mins. Communication 15 mins. Test 5 mins. Total 55 mins.

A ANALYSIS

This unit looks at the determiners above and the confusion often caused by them. The confusion is usually caused by the fact that the meaning of these words (in terms of affirmative and negative) is often distinct from their grammatical form, for example, *every* has a plural meaning but takes a singular verb. The exercises in this section look at both form and meaning. Allow about twenty minutes to do the exercises and another five or so for discussion and feedback.

1 *Answers:*

		letter
a	[T]	A, B, C, D, E, F
b	[T]	A, B
c	[T]	E, F
d	[F]	
e	[F]	
f	[T]	C, D, E, F
g	[T]	A, B
h	[F]	
i	[T]	E, F
j	[F]	
k	[F]	
l	[F]	

2 *Answers:* see above.

3 Make sure the students understand the concept of *singular* and *dual* before doing this exercise.

Answers:

	verb		focus		number		
	sing	plural	affirm	neg	sing	dual	more than 2
all		✓	✓				✓
both		✓	✓			✓	
each	✓		✓		✓		
every	✓		✓				✓
neither	✓			✓		✓	
none	✓			✓			✓

Make sure that the students understand that it is possible to have a singular verb with a plural meaning (with *every*) or a dual meaning (with *neither*). It is useful also to point out that *none* and *neither* are always followed by the partitive (*of*), that *all, both* and *each* can stand on their own or be followed by the partitive, and that *every* always stands on its own. This unit does not introduce *either*, so it might be worth mentioning its use to the students, i.e. it is used in questions and in sentences where the verb is in the negative, e.g. *Are either of you coming?* and *I can't see either of them.*

4 *Answers:*
- **d** Both girls on court 2 are wearing skirts.
- **e** One of the girls is wearing glasses.
- **f** Both of the girls on court 3 are wearing black T-shirts.
- **h** Neither of the boys is wearing black shoes; both of them are wearing white shoes.
- **j** One of the players is hitting the ball.
- **k** All of the girls are wearing black T-shirts.
- **l** None of the girls is sitting down.

B PRACTICE

These two exercises are straightforward and should only take a few minutes.

5 *Answers:*
- **a** None of the ... is
- **b** All (of) ... have
- **c** None of ... is
- **d** Each ... is/or every ... is
- **e** Neither ... is
- **f** Each/or every ... is

6 *Answers:*
- **a** Both of the dresses are on dummies.
- **b** All of the T-shirts have short sleeves/are on the left.
- **c** None of the dummies is wearing shorts/T-shirts.
- **d** Neither of the skirts is on the floor.
- **e** Each pair of shorts is on the right.
- **f** Both short-sleeved blouses are on the dummies.
- **g** Every long-sleeved blouse is on the floor.
- **h** Both pairs of shorts have belts.

C COMMUNICATION

7 This exercise really requires two copies of the picture. If you can, it is worth taking an extra copy of this page for each student, otherwise allow a little extra time for the activity as the students will have to make a rough copy of the picture.

Follow this procedure:
- Ask the students to make a very rough copy of the picture if necessary.
- Explain to the students that they have to change the picture to make it individual, by using colours, or stars, stripes, patterns etc. Give them a few minutes to do this.
- In pairs, each student describes his/her picture to his/her partner, using *all, both, each* etc. For example, *All of the T-shirts are green; both pairs of shorts are striped.*
- The students listen and follow their partner's instructions to complete their spare picture. Then the students check their pictures with their partners.

D TEST

Allow only a few minutes for this test and for checking. Give the students marks out of ten.

8 *Answers:*
- **a** Both **b** None **c** Every **d** Neither **e** all **f** Each **g** Both **h** all **i** neither **j** none

FURTHER PRACTICE

No further practice for this unit.

My secret desire
Wish + would or wish + past simple?

LESSON PLAN

Aim: To distinguish between and practise the use of *wish + past simple* to express regret about a situation and a wish for it to be different, and the use of *wish + would + infinitive* to express a desire for an action to take place by someone or something else to change a present situation.

Topic: Private desires, wishes and regrets.

Lesson phases: Analysis and feedback 10 mins. Practice 15 mins. Game 15 mins. Test 10 mins. Total 50 mins.

A ANALYSIS

Allow five minutes for each exercise.

1 *Answers:*

Carla	I wish I was a rock star.
Jim	I wish Carla would marry me.
Maria	I wish my teacher would give me a grade A.
Tom	I wish I was a millionaire.
Teacher	I wish I was on holiday.

2 *Answers:*

Regret about a situation
I wish I was a rock star.
I wish I was a millionaire.
I wish I was on holiday.
I wish + subject + past simple

Desire for an action by someone else.
I wish Carla would marry me.
I wish my teacher would give me a grade A.
I wish + subject + would + infinitive

Check that students are clear about the distinction between the two forms with *I wish*.
You may like to point out the alternative form used to express regret, e.g.
I wish I *were* a rock star.
I wish I *were* a millionaire.
This has been traditionally taught as the correct form but the use of the past simple (*was* with all singular persons) is nowadays more usual in everyday speech.

B PRACTICE

Allow six or seven minutes for each exercise.

3 *Answers:*
a (i) **b** (ii) **c** (ii) **d** (ii) **e** (i) **f** (ii) **g** (ii) **h** (i)

4 *Answers:*
  a I wish the government would reduce taxes.
  b I wish I was a teacher.
  c I wish I was a film director.
  d I wish rich countries would help poor ones.
  e I wish my uncle would teach me to drive.
  f I wish my English was better.

C GAME

Allow up to fifteen minutes for the game – the amount of time will depend on the size of the class.

5 Read through the instructions with the class. Follow this procedure:
  • Students write their sentences on pieces of paper.
  • Teacher collects pieces of paper.
  • Teacher jumbles up the papers and hands them out to students.
  • Students guess whose paper they have received and write a name on the back of the paper.
  • Teacher collects pieces of paper again.
  • Teacher hands out each paper to the student whose name appears on the back.
  • Students in turn read out the sentences written on the paper they have been given. Teacher asks class to decide if the paper really belongs to the student reading out the sentences.

D TEST

Allow ten minutes for completion of the exercise and checking.

6 *Answers:*
  a would stop
  b was
  c was
  d would do
  e would get
  f lived
  g would make
  h had
  i was
  j would cook

FURTHER PRACTICE

EGU   Exs 37.3, 39.1, 39.2

Students'
Material

The following 30 lessons may be

photocopied for classroom use.

Problem students

Present simple or present continuous?

A   ANALYSIS

TEACHER'S REPORT ..... Sandy Girton

Sandy is a student in class 3F. This term she is studying English, mathematics, general science and history. I hope that next term she will also take geography and art.

Unfortunately Sandy's work is very poor, and I think this is because she misses so many lessons. I know that she enjoys English and general science, and she usually comes to my history class. The reason for her truancy may be her parents. Apparently Mrs Girton has left her husband and is living in a hotel. So Sandy's father expects her to stay at home and do the cooking and cleaning in her mother's place. I have written to Mr Girton and at the moment I am waiting for him to phone me.

M.J. Hughes.

1   All schools have some problem students. Sandy Girton is a typical example. Her work isn't very good and she often misses lessons. Her teacher has written a report about her for the school principal:

Discuss these questions.

  a   Why has Sandy's teacher written a report?
  b   Does Sandy hate going to school?
  c   What do you think is the reason for her problems?
  d   What would you do if you were Sandy's teacher?

2   In English there are some important differences between the uses of the present simple and present continuous tenses. Study the phrases from Sandy's report and tick the correct column for the type of meaning, then write the tense we use in the boxes at the bottom.

	permanent situation	temporary situation	habit or repeated action	general truth or fact	action happening now
a I am waiting for him to phone me.	[ ]	[ ]	[ ]	[ ]	[ ]
b She usually comes to my history class.	[ ]	[ ]	[ ]	[ ]	[ ]
c All schools have some problem students.	[ ]	[ ]	[ ]	[ ]	[ ]
d Her mother is living in a hotel.	[ ]	[ ]	[ ]	[ ]	[ ]
e Sandy is a student.	[ ]	[ ]	[ ]	[ ]	[ ]
f She enjoys English.	[ ]	[ ]	[ ]	[ ]	[ ]
g She often misses lessons.	[ ]	[ ]	[ ]	[ ]	[ ]
h This term she is studying English.	[ ]	[ ]	[ ]	[ ]	[ ]
present simple or ***present continuous tense?***					

B PRACTICE

3 Complete these sentences by putting the verb/s in brackets into the correct tense/s.

  a My brother usually (work) _____ as an engineer but at the moment he (study) _____ for an extra qualification.

  b There was a fire at my friend's house so he (stay) _____ at a hotel until the damage is repaired.

  c My father (be) _____ taller than my mother.

  d Marion always (arrive) _____ late on Fridays.

  e I think smoking is unhealthy so now I (try) _____ to give up.

  f Can you hear the birds? They (sing) _____!

  g I usually (like) _____ eating, but tonight I (not enjoy) _____ the food at all.

  h 50% of British families (keep) _____ pets.

4 These sentences contain mistakes. Find the mistakes and write the correct version.

  a My grandmother is living in a cottage, she has lived there all her life.

  _____

  b Statistics show that the Dutch are being the tallest race.

  _____

  c I'm Spanish. I'm coming from Madrid.

  _____

  d Look! That woman tries to jump on the bus.

  _____

  e The state of Florida is having a sub-tropical climate.

  _____

C COMMUNICATION

5 *Student A:* You have decided to spend two weeks on a summer course at Somerby College. Look at the brochure and tick the options you prefer.

SOMERBY COLLEGE   Summer course programme

Please tick your choices
STUDY SUBJECTS
Computing [ ] Painting [ ] English [ ] Russian [ ]
Dancing [ ] Music [ ] Drama [ ] Gardening [ ]

SPORTS TUITION
Archery [ ] Tennis [ ] Waterskiiing [ ] Sailing [ ]
Horseriding [ ] Canoeing [ ] Fencing [ ] Shooting [ ]

ACCOMMODATION
With local family [ ] Hotel [ ] College dormitory [ ]

MEALS
In college refectory [ ] In hotel restaurant [ ]
Self-catering [ ]

EVENING ACTIVITIES
Video club [ ] Discos [ ] Theatre club [ ]
Cordon Bleu club [ ]

You are now in the middle of the course at Somerby. Your partner interviews you.

Student B: You are the research officer at Somerby Residential College. It is your job to investigate the background and interests of the students at the college. Your partner is now in the middle of a course. Interview him/her and complete the questionnaire.

SOMERBY RESIDENTIAL COLLEGE	STUDENT QUESTIONNAIRE	
	AT HOME	AT SOMERBY
SUBJECTS STUDIED:	_____	_____
SPORTS ACTIVITIES:	_____	_____
TYPE OF ACCOMMODATION:	_____	_____
MEALS:	_____	_____
EVENING ACTIVITIES:	_____	_____

D TEST

6 Choose the correct verb form to fill the gaps.

  a Sheila is in hospital for a month, she _____ from an operation.
  (i) is recovering   (ii) recovers

  b I've just started university. I _____ a Physics degree.
  (i) am taking   (ii) take

  c The United Nations _____ its headquarters in New York.
  (i) is having   (ii) has

  d I _____ my bicycle while my car is being repaired.
  (i) am using   (ii) use

  e My parents always _____ to the theatre on Friday nights.
  (i) are going   (ii) go

  f Oh look! That tiny cat _____ that big dog!
  (i) is chasing   (ii) chases

  g Everyone in our family _____ blond hair and blue eyes.
  (i) is having   (ii) has

  h Our teacher is ill today so we _____ a day off school.
  (i) are having   (ii) have

  i Carol usually doesn't eat very much but today she _____ a feast!
  (i) is having   (ii) has

  j I often _____ television in the evenings.
  (i) am watching   (ii) watch

Stop thief!

Past simple or past continuous?

A ANALYSIS

1 Complete the captions for the story with suitable verbs in the past simple tense. The pictures are not in the correct order.

   a It was pouring with rain one day and Penny was bored. She _____ to bake some cakes but _____ that her cupboard was empty, so she _____ to go to the shop.

   b She _____ into her car and _____ to the shop.

   c She _____ the car and _____ into the shop, but she _____ to lock the car door.

   d As she was waiting to pay for her shopping, she _____ out of the window. Someone was trying to steal her car!

   e She _____ out of the shop but her car was already disappearing down the road.

   f She _____ for her shopping and _____ to the police station.

   g She was waiting to talk to a police officer at the desk and she was looking out of the window, when she _____ her car arrive.

   h A policeman _____ into the station with a young man and said, 'I almost crashed into him while he was driving at seventy through the High Street! I think it's a stolen car!'

2 Now put the pictures and captions in the correct order.

   a _____   b _____   c _____   d _____

   e _____   f _____   g _____   h _____

3 Go through the story and underline all the verbs in the past continuous tense (*was -ing*).

4 The completed story shows a number of different uses of the past simple and the past continuous. Complete the chart like the examples given.

	examples	past simple	past cont.
Sequence of events in the past.	got, drove	✓	
Background information to a narrative.	was pouring		✓
An action which interrupts another.			
An action which is interrupted by another.			
Two actions taking place at the same time.			

Which words can introduce an interrupted action? _____

Which word can introduce an interrupting action? _____

B PRACTICE

5 Fill the gaps in these sentences with a suitable verb in either the past simple or the past continuous.

a Jane _____ the washing up when she _____ the news.

b John _____ his work for the evening and then he _____ to bed.

c It was a typical winter's day: snow _____ and people _____ their hats and gloves.

d He _____ his leg while he _____ to catch the bus.

e They _____ the game of chess they _____, then they _____ the house and _____ to the local wine bar, where they _____ their friends.

f While he _____ to the conference centre he _____ the speech he had written.

6 Join the two halves of the sentences below.

a They were listening to music

b As he was reading the paper

c They drove to the station

d The chimney was gently smoking

e The dog bit the child's hand

1 as she was stroking it.

2 when they noticed the thief.

3 and the door was swinging on its hinges.

4 he was making notes about the share prices.

5 then they left the car and took the train.

C COMMUNICATION

7 Work in pairs, A and B.

Student A: look at pictures 1 to 3 below.
Student B: look at pictures 4 to 6 below.
Make notes about your pictures in order to be able to describe the story of each one (you are the young man in the pictures). Tell your partner about each picture, using the past, then put the pictures in the correct order and retell the story in full.

D TEST

8 Complete the sentences below with the verbs in brackets, using either the past simple or the past continuous tense.

a The television _____ a strange noise all last night while I _____ it. (make, watch)

b The Chinese vase _____ off the table and _____ as it hit the hard floor. (fall, shatter)

c She _____ the road when the car _____ her. (cross, hit)

d The day _____ and the birds _____ in the trees. (dawn, sing)

e I _____ a really good sleep until you _____ me. (have, disturb)

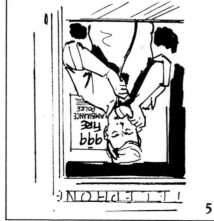

European Community

Past simple or present perfect?

A ANALYSIS

1 Look carefully at these sentences and decide if they are grammatically correct (✔) or not (✘).

a Spain joined the EEC in 1987. [ ]
b Greece has been a member of the EEC since 1987. [ ]
c Spain is a member of the EEC since 1987. [ ]
d Greece has joined the EEC in 1987. [ ]
e Turkey hasn't joined the EEC yet. [ ]
f France joined the EEC for many years. [ ]
g Denmark was a member of the EEC since 1973. [ ]
h Denmark became a member of the EEC in 1973. [ ]
i The EEC has recently harmonised its employment laws after many years of negotiation. [ ]
j Britain has disputed EEC policy on several occasions. [ ]

2 a Match each of the correct sentences from exercise 1 with one of the explanations below, and write the sentence letter(s) on the lines below.

b Which tense (or tenses) do we use for each type of sentence? Tick the correct box below.

which sentences	*present perfect*	*past simple*
A an action or situation in the past where the exact time is given _____	[ ]	[ ]
B an action or situation in the past when either the action or the situation or the time period is still continuing (this can also refer to a negative action or situation) _____	[ ]	[ ]
C an action or situation which started in the past and finished very recently _____	[ ]	[ ]
D a series of repeated actions in the past which may continue into the present _____	[ ]	[ ]

B PRACTICE

3 Put the verb in brackets in the correct tense. You may have to change the word order.

a Ireland (be) a member of the EEC since 1973.
b I never (visit) Paris but I (go) to Versailles last year.
c British Airways just (announce) a new fare to Moscow.
d Peter (not finish) his homework yet.
e Maria ever (see) a bullfight?

On the map: UNITED KINGDOM, DENMARK, NETHERLANDS, REPUBLIC OF IRELAND, BELGIUM, GERMANY, LUXEMBOURG, PORTUGAL, FRANCE, SPAIN, ITALY, TURKEY, GREECE

LESSON 3

40

4 Sam works as an errand boy for Mrs Briggs. Mrs Briggs is very bossy. Every morning she gives Sam a list of things to do. This is the list she gave Sam this morning:

It is now five o'clock and Sam is telling Mrs Briggs about the things he has (or hasn't) done yet. Sam has made notes on the list of errands to remind him. What does Sam say to Mrs Briggs? Write four sentences using the past simple and four sentences using the present perfect.

C COMMUNICATION

5 Complete the questionnaire by asking your partner questions. Your partner should then complete his/ her questionnaire by asking you questions.

Compare your answers with another pair. What are the most common types of holiday, transport and accommodation in your group?

As a group, discuss the three topics under these headings.

the most enjoyable   *the most unusual*
the best value   *the cheapest*
the most expensive   *the most exciting*

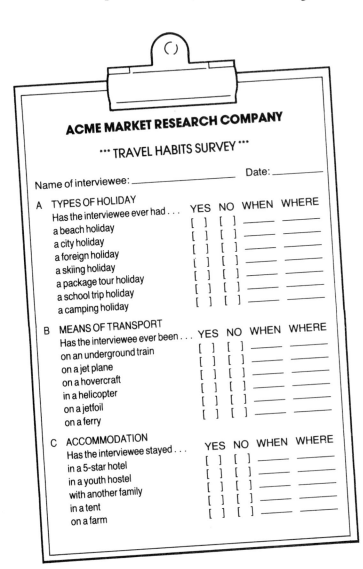

OPEN MAIL ✓   *at half past nine*
BUY 100 ENVELOPES ✓
TAKE THE PARCELS TO THE POST OFFICE ✓ *before coffee time*
MAKE COFFEE FOR THE SECRETARIES ✓ *at 11 o'clock*
TAKE THE NEW FAX MACHINE TO THE BASEMENT ✓ *at 2 o'clock*
BUY A BIRTHDAY CARD FOR JULIE ✗
REPLACE THE LIGHT BULBS IN THE RECEPTION AREA ✗
COLLECT THE PAY CHEQUES FROM MR GRIFFITHS ✓

ACME MARKET RESEARCH COMPANY

*** TRAVEL HABITS SURVEY ***

Name of interviewee: _____   Date: _____

A TYPES OF HOLIDAY Has the interviewee ever had . . .	YES	NO	WHEN	WHERE
a beach holiday	[ ]	[ ]	___	___
a city holiday	[ ]	[ ]	___	___
a foreign holiday	[ ]	[ ]	___	___
a skiing holiday	[ ]	[ ]	___	___
a package tour holiday	[ ]	[ ]	___	___
a school trip holiday	[ ]	[ ]	___	___
a camping holiday	[ ]	[ ]	___	___

B MEANS OF TRANSPORT Has the interviewee ever been . . .	YES	NO	WHEN	WHERE
on an underground train	[ ]	[ ]	___	___
on a jet plane	[ ]	[ ]	___	___
on a hovercraft	[ ]	[ ]	___	___
in a helicopter	[ ]	[ ]	___	___
on a jetfoil	[ ]	[ ]	___	___
on a ferry	[ ]	[ ]	___	___

C ACCOMMODATION Has the interviewee stayed . . .	YES	NO	WHEN	WHERE
in a 5-star hotel	[ ]	[ ]	___	___
in a youth hostel	[ ]	[ ]	___	___
with another family	[ ]	[ ]	___	___
in a tent	[ ]	[ ]	___	___
on a farm	[ ]	[ ]	___	___

D TEST

6 Choose the correct word/s to fill the gaps.

a There are twelve members of the EEC; most _____ in 1958.
(i) have joined   (ii) joined   (iii) already joined

b There's a new play on in London. It _____ at the Theatre Royal.
(i) has just opened   (ii) has opened   (iii) opened

c I wrote an essay last night, but I _____ time to type it yet.
(i) didn't have   (ii) haven't had   (iii) don't have

d The population of London increased dramatically until 1945, but since then it _____ considerably.
(i) has decreased   (ii) decreased
(iii) is decreasing

e Children _____ the right to vote, and they probably never will.
(i) never had   (ii) have never had
(iii) didn't have

f Many countries are poor; some of them _____ for many years.
(i) are   (ii) were   (iii) have been

g I have taken the driving test four times; the last time _____ in March.
(i) was   (ii) is   (iii) has been

h That meal was wonderful! I _____ such delicious chicken!
(i) never had   (ii) have never had
(iii) haven't had

i I wish I could get a job. I _____ for so many.
(i) applied   (ii) had applied   (iii) have applied

j She is still young, but she _____ a lot in her short life.
(i) has achieved   (ii) achieves   (iii) achieved

What have you been doing?

Present perfect simple or present perfect continuous?

A ANALYSIS

1 Match the captions with the pictures.

                                                picture

- **a** I've spent all my money. I'm broke. _____
- **b** That's the last one. I've typed twenty letters! _____
- **c** I've been eating those cakes you made. They're wonderful! _____
- **d** I've been typing letters since nine o'clock this morning. _____
- **e** I've been spending lots of money! _____
- **f** I've eaten all the cakes and I feel really ill! _____

2 Now match the captions and pictures with these questions.

                                            caption   *picture*

- **a** What have you been doing in the kitchen? _____ _____
- **b** Why can't you afford to come with us tonight? _____ _____
- **c** What have you been doing at the shops? _____ _____
- **d** You look awful – what's wrong? _____ _____
- **e** Have you finished those letters yet? _____ _____
- **f** Haven't you done my report yet? What have you been doing all morning? _____ _____

3 The sentences in exercise 1 focus on different aspects of the action – its duration, the result of the action or the number of times the action has been done. Look at the captions to the pictures and complete this chart (only four captions go here):

	caption
Duration	
Result	
Number	

Two captions are left which do not focus on any of these. Which are they? They focus on the action itself.

4 Now complete these sentences, using *present perfect simple* or *present perfect continuous*.

- **a** When we want to focus on the action itself, we use the

  _____

  _____

- **b** When we want to focus on the result of the action, we use the

  _____

  _____

- **c** When we want to focus on the duration of the action, we use the

  _____

  _____

- **d** When we want to focus on the number of times the action has been done, we use the

  _____

B PRACTICE

5 Choose an ending from these to complete the sentences below.

at least twice	for half an hour
for days	ten times

a I've been watching television _____

b I've told you this _____

c I've been knocking at the door _____

d We've stayed here _____

e I've knocked at the door _____

f He's been saying that _____

g We've been staying at this hotel _____

h He's said that _____

6 Match these sentences with the questions below them, then complete them with a suitable verb in the present perfect simple or continuous.

a She's _____ at that school for ten years.

b Yes, he's _____ the driving test four times.

c I've already _____ three cups of tea, thanks.

d I've _____ in my flat all week.

e No, someone's _____ all the pencils in the shop.

1 Is he still learning to drive?

2 Where have you been all week – I haven't seen you for ages?

3 Has she been at the school for a long time?

4 Do you have any pencils, please?

5 Would you like a cup of coffee?

C COMMUNICATION

7 Work in pairs.

Student A: You are a market researcher working for Brickwood Leisure Centre. Interview your partner to find out how much he/she has used the Centre over the last year and why he/she has used certain facilities and not others. Use questions like these:

Have you been using the swimming pool?

How often have you used it?

Why haven't you been using the library?

Write the answers in the form.

Student B: You are being interviewed about your use of the Leisure Centre. Be prepared to answer questions about your use of the different facilities shown on the form and to give reasons why you have or haven't used different facilities.

BRICKWOOD LEISURE CENTRE

Dear Member

Our records show that you have been a member of Brickwood Leisure Centre for one year now. In order to maintain our high standards and provide a better service we are conducting a survey into the facilities used by our members. We would be grateful if you would answer the questions below and return this form to us. Thank you.

Name ....

Membership no. ....

Date of joining ....

Our facilities:

Facilities used	yes	no	frequency			
			daily	weekly	monthly	once/twice in past year
swimming pool						
fitness studio						
indoor tennis						
badminton						
table tennis						
library						
cafeteria						
aerobics classes						
language classes						
art classes						
dance classes						
computer workshop						

D TEST

8 Write **pps** (present perfect simple) or **ppc** (present perfect continuous) after each sentence and fill the gap with a suitable verb.

a I've _____ three European countries. _____

b I've never _____ any live concerts. _____

c I've _____ less alcohol recently. _____

d I haven't _____ very hard this morning. _____

e I haven't _____ any films for a long time. _____

f I've _____ tennis since I was a child. _____

g Has he really _____ all those biscuits? _____

h She's delighted because she's just _____ me at chess! _____

i The doctor's _____ me some pills . . . _____

j . . . because I haven't _____ very well recently. _____

Witness to crime

Past simple or past perfect?

A ANALYSIS

STATEMENT OF WITNESS

NAME OF WITNESS: Albert Pearson

WITNESSING OFFICER: P.C. McLintock 90776

form CID 91/45 REF: b33–16

My name is Albert Pearson. I am the manager of the National Provident Bank in Wormsley Street.

On Friday 20 June I returned home at five o'clock. I immediately knew something was wrong because the lock on the front door had been broken. I called to my wife but heard no answer so I walked upstairs to the bedroom. As I walked into the room somebody shut the door behind me. My wife was sitting on the bed. She had been tied up. There were two men in the room. They told me that unless I took them to the bank and opened the safe they would kill my wife. Of course I had no choice but to obey them.

Normally I wouldn't be able to open the safe on my own because there are two keys; the other key is kept by my assistant, Julie Wesley. But earlier that morning Ms Wesley had come into my office and told me that her mother was seriously ill, and she had to visit her, so she had asked me to keep her key until she returned after the weekend. I took the two men to the bank and opened the safe. They tied me up and locked me in. For some reason the electronic alarm did not sound, so obviously somebody had turned it off before we arrived. Usually Ms Wesley checks that it is turned on as she is the last person to leave.

I was discovered by the cleaners on Monday morning.

signed

A. Pearson

1 Read the statement. Who do you think planned the bank robbery? The police need to work out what happened on Friday. Put the events into the correct time sequence:

a Mr Pearson walked upstairs to the bedroom.

b Two men broke into Mr Pearson's house.

c Mr Pearson was discovered by the cleaners.

d Mr Pearson took the men to the bank.

e Julie told Mr Pearson about her mother's illness.

f Mrs Pearson was tied up.

g Mr Pearson opened the safe.

h Mr Pearson went home at five o'clock.

i Mr Pearson was locked in the safe.

2 Study the witness statement. Find an example for each of these descriptions and decide which tense we use.

a to talk about something which happened at a specific time in the past

e.g. _____

b to talk about something which happened at a specific time in the past but before something else in the past

e.g. _____

c to talk about something which happened at an unspecified time in the past before something else in the past

e.g. _____

past simple	past perfect

B PRACTICE

3 Choose the best verb form to fill the gaps in these sentences.

   a My grandfather hated retirement because he
   _____ so busy when he was working.
   (i) had been   (ii) was

   b I should have arrived earlier, the food _____
   by the time I got there.
   (i) had already been eaten   (ii) was already eaten

   c I'm exhausted. I _____ all the way from the station.
   (i) had run   (ii) ran

   d Juan married very young, but he _____ his
   wife since childhood.
   (i) had known   (ii) knew

   e The house feels cold even though I _____ the
   heating this morning.
   (i) had turned on   (ii) turned on

4 Write sentences like these examples.
   7.15 post arrived
   7.30 I got up
   I got up after the post had arrived.
   8.30 I arrived at cinema
   8.30 film started
   When I arrived at the cinema the film started.

   a 9.25   Shop closed.
   9.40   I arrived.

   b March   I passed the driving test.
   April   I bought my first car.

   c 1987   We sold our house.
   1987   We bought a farm.

   d June   I graduated from college.
   July   I started working.

   e 9.30   Jim finished eating dessert.
   9.30   The waiter brought the bill.

THE DAILY NEWS

STUDENT MURDERED!

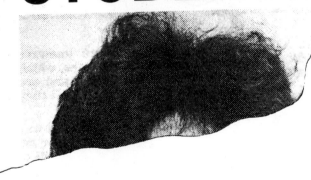

C COMMUNICATION

5 'Alibis'

Last night, sometime between six o'clock and nine o'clock, a student was murdered in your school.

The police want to know what everybody was doing at that time yesterday – anybody without a good alibi will be arrested!

Work in pairs. Talk with your partner and decide what you were doing together between six and nine last night. Check that you both agree on all the exact details.

One of you will have to wait outside the classroom while the class interviews the other. If there are any differences between your answers you could be the murderer!

D TEST

6 Complete the sentences by putting the verbs in brackets into the past simple or past perfect tense:

   a When I arrived home the TV was missing.
   Someone (steal) _____ it.

   b I was late for the flight. When I arrived it (already leave) _____ .

   c Joyce is still hungry, even though she (eat)
   _____ a big lunch earlier.

   d I didn't know the man. I (never see) _____ him
   before.

   e Ann didn't want to visit the theatre because she
   (see) _____ the play already.

   f Mrs Greville (return) _____ to work after her
   children had grown up.

   g I'm feeling rather tired because I (stay up)
   _____ very late last night.

   h Jimmy was nervous when he visited the dentist
   because he (have) _____ two fillings on his
   previous visit.

   i When I returned to the hotel my room looked
   much tidier because the maid (make) _____
   the bed.

   j I'm starving! I (not have) _____ any breakfast
   this morning.

Changes

Used to do or be used to doing?

A ANALYSIS

Reporter I'm here in Grassbanks Prison to talk to a few prisoners. Let's start with Barry Stephens. Barry, you've been here for over ten years. How has your life changed in that time?

Stephens Well, look at me now; *I'm old and unhealthy. I didn't use to be like this. I used to be totally different: active, I used to play a lot of sport, and handsome ...*

Reporter Are you married?

Stephens I used to be, but my wife divorced me.

Reporter So what did you do? Why are you in prison?

Stephens *I robbed a bank.* I was really stupid!

Reporter How do you feel about prison now?

Stephens Well, after a while you get used to it. *I'm used to being in this cell now, and I'm used to doing just ten minutes exercise every day,* but it doesn't mean that I like it.

1 Look at the pictures around Barry. In some of them he is thinking about the past, and in others he is thinking about the present. Which ones are past and which are present?

past _____ *present* _____

46

2 Now look at his words and concentrate on the phrases in italics. What do the phrases express? Match them with their meanings, as in the example:

a I *used to be* handsome. **5**
b I *used to play* a lot of sport.
c I *robbed* a bank.
d I'*m used to being* in this cell.
e I'*m used to doing* ten minutes' exercise every day.

1 single action in the past
2 repeated action in the present
3 continuous state in the present
4 repeated action in the past
5 continuous state in the past

3 Now decide how we express these ideas about the past and present:

a single action in the past   <u>past simple</u>
b repeated action in the past   _____
c continuous state in the past   _____
d continuous state in the present   _____
(to which one has become accustomed)
e repeated action in the present   _____

4 Decide whether the following sentences about Barry are true (T) or false (F).

a He's used to going out with his wife and children. [ ]
b He used to be very active. [ ]
c He's not used to being in a cell. [ ]
d He didn't use to play a lot of sport. [ ]
e He used to spend a lot of time reading on his own. [ ]
f He's used to eating awful prison food. [ ]

What do you notice about the negative of *used to*?
Now correct the false sentences.

B PRACTICE

5 Complete these eight sentences about Barry's thoughts, using the verbs in brackets.

a He (go out) _____ with his friends.
b He (live) _____ in a small cell.
c He (play) _____ table tennis with other prisoners.
d He (lead) _____ an adventurous life.
e He (have) _____ a wife and two children.
f He (eat) _____ prison food.
g He (watch) _____ crime films on the television.
h He (be) _____ very handsome.

6 Write these sentences in full from the prompts.

a When he was free Barry/do/exercise but now he/do/very little.

_____

b When I was a child I/ride/bicycle but now I/drive/car.

_____

c When my brother was in the army he/get/up/very early but now he/lie/bed/late in the morning.

_____

d When I was at school I/do/homework/evenings but now I/watch television/evenings.

_____

C COMMUNICATION

7 Work in groups of four or five. Imagine a situation where your life has changed drastically. (Your teacher will give you some ideas if you can't think of anything.)

Write four short sentences about your situation, two describing what you used to be/do, and two describing what you are used to doing. Read your sentences to your group. They try to guess what has happened to you.

Example:
I used to live with my parents.
I used to go to school.
Now I'm used to living in a room on my own.
I'm used to reading lots of books and writing essays.
(I've just gone to college/university in a different town.)

D TEST

8 Fill in the gaps in this paragraph with a suitable verb, using (*not*) *used to do* or *be used to doing*.

A hundred years ago life was very different. People were either very rich or very poor. They (**a**) _____ electricity in their homes and many people (**b**) _____ in very hard and very dirty jobs. While today we (**c**) _____ at college or university, and then we have a choice in what jobs we do, people then (**d**) _____ able to choose their work. Because we have such good transport today we (**e**) _____ quite long distances to work, but people in the past (**f**) _____ very close to their work. People then (**g**) _____ from one town to another to find work, either. There (**h**) _____ a lot of illness and people quite often (**i**) _____ from illnesses which we can treat very easily today. We (**j**) _____ very good treatment from doctors, and we have access to good hospitals if necessary.

We're going to have a good time!

Ways of expressing the future

A ANALYSIS

Cathy This is the life! *¹I'm going to stay here all afternoon.*

Alice What! *²You'll get bored within half an hour!* You know what you're like!

Cathy No, I won't. I love lazing around like this. Alice, do you fancy seeing a film tonight?

Alice *³But we're having dinner with those two guys* we met on Monday. Don't you remember?

Cathy Oh yes. What time?

Alice *⁴We're meeting them at half past eight* at that fish restaurant near the hotel. OK?

Cathy Mmm. *⁵I think I'll have a swim.* (later) Brrr. The water's freezing!

Alice Why don't you wait until we get back to the hotel? *⁶The pool will be a lot warmer than the sea.*

Cathy Yes, but *⁷I'm going to get burnt* if I stay here; it's so hot.

Alice I doubt it. Look at those clouds. *⁸I think it's going to rain.* Still, let's enjoy it while we can. Oh damn! I've forgotten the sun oil!

Cathy *⁹I'll go and get some.* I could do with the walk, anyway. I'm getting bored.

Alice Don't forget *¹⁰the bus leaves at five thirty ...*

1 Answer these questions about the dialogue.

  a How long does Cathy intend to stay on the beach?
  b What is Alice's response to Cathy's intention?
  c What arrangements have they made for the evening?
  d What does Alice say about the hotel pool?
  e Why does Alice think it's going to rain?
  f What does Cathy decide to do?

2 Which of the phrases in italics in the dialogue express the following ideas?
Some examples are given for you.
intention to do something _____
a decision made at the time of speaking ___5___
an arrangement already made ___3___
a prediction about someone/something ___2___
a statement about the future based on firm evidence in the present ___7___
something on a timetable/schedule _____

3 Now complete the following chart about the sentences.

3 Now complete the following chart about the sentences.

	expresses	*will*	*present continuous*	*going to*	*present simple*
a I'm going to stay here	intention			✓	
b You'll get bored	prediction	✓			
c ... we're having dinner					
d We're meeting them at half past eight					
e I think I'll have a swim.					
f The pool will be warmer					
g I'm going to get burnt.					
h I think it's going to rain.					
i I'll go and get some.					
j ... the bus leaves at five thirty.					

B PRACTICE

4 Complete the gaps in this dialogue with the correct form of the future.

A Have you booked a holiday for this summer yet?

B Yes. We (**a**) _____ (spend) a week in the Algarve. We (**b**) _____ (stay) in a villa near the beach.

A Lovely. It sounds really relaxing.

B Yes. My son is bringing a friend, so we hope that they (**c**) _____ (keep) each other amused. At least, that's the intention. If so, Gary and I (**d**) _____ (sunbathe) all day and in the evening we (**e**) _____ (try out) all the local restaurants. What about you?

A Well, John and I booked some time ago; we (**f**) _____ (sail) round the Greek islands.

B Mmm. Sounds good.

A Yes, but our plane (**g**) _____ (leave) on Tuesday, and there (**h**) _____ (be) delays – the strike has already started!

B Oh no! Still, it's only Thursday now. I'm sure they (**i**) _____ (not be) on strike after the weekend and the delays (**j**) _____ (not be) too bad.

5 Write one sentence to show what each of the people is saying, using the correct form of the future.

a _____

b _____

c _____

d _____

e _____

f _____

C COMMUNICATION

6 Below are a number of questions. Think about these questions in relation to your own future and make notes according to plans you have already made, your intentions and any predictions you may have. Then discuss them in groups of four, remembering that you can change your mind and make spontaneous decisions.

Immediate future:
What are you having for dinner tonight?
When's your next night out?
What are you doing at the weekend?
Are you going on holiday this year?
When are you next going to the cinema or theatre?

Distant future:
Are you going to travel? Where?
Do you wish to study further?
Do you intend to change your job?
Do you intend to buy a house/move?
Do you think you'll ever go to prison?
Do you think you'll ever visit the moon?

D TEST

7 Choose the correct tense for each sentence.

a This exam is very important. I _____ very hard to pass it.
(i) try   (ii) am going to try   (iii) will try

b My brother _____ on 1 April – it's all arranged.
(i) is getting married   (ii) gets married   (iii) will get married

c I'm very tired. I think I _____ for a while.
(i) am going to lie down   (ii) lie down   (iii) will lie down

d Look at what your friend's eating; he _____ really ill!
(i) is going to be   (ii) is being   (iii) is

e What time do you get to the resort? – Well, the plane _____ at seven thirty.
(i) is going to land   (ii) will land   (iii) lands

f They're not suited at all. I think they _____ within a year.
(i) will be divorced   (ii) are getting divorced   (iii) get divorced

g Your homework looks really difficult; I _____ you.
(i) help   (ii) will help   (iii) am helping

h Hurry up! The bus _____ in five minutes!
(i) is leaving   (ii) is going to leave   (iii) leaves

i Are you free tomorrow? No, I _____ Bob for lunch.
(i) am meeting   (ii) will meet   (iii) meet

j My little sister says that she _____ from now on!
(i) is behaving   (ii) is going to behave   (iii) behaves

49

Sports day

Can, could, be able to

A ANALYSIS

Dialogue 1
Two girls talking on the phone.

Jenny   Hi, Lucy, it's me. I'm ringing to ask you about the sports day.

Lucy   Oh, yes. When is it?

Jenny   Next Sunday. *¹Can you come?*

Lucy   Um, I'm not sure. Hang on a moment, let me ask my mum. (aside) Mum, *²can I go to the sports day* with Jenny next Sunday? ... Hi, Jenny. No, *³I can't come.* We're going to visit my grandmother that day. Sorry.

Jenny   Oh, that's a real shame. Everyone else is going, and, well, you know *⁴you can swim so well*, you'd easily win for us.

Lucy   Oh, *⁵I can't swim that well*, and *⁶I certainly can't run at all.* Anyway, if you ring me when you get back *⁷you'll be able to tell me* all about it.

Dialogue 2
Next week, on the phone again.

Jenny   Lucy, it's me. I've just got home from the sports day.

Lucy   Oh, how was it?

Jenny   Great! It was a real pity *⁸you couldn't come.*

Lucy   Who won the swimming?

Jenny   Someone from the other school, I'm afraid. Alison tried really hard, but *⁹she wasn't able to keep up.*

Lucy   What about the running? *¹⁰Mark can run really fast, can't he?*

Jenny   Well, *¹¹he was just able to finish third ...*

1   Read the two dialogues and answer the questions.
   a   Can Lucy go to the sports day? Why/why not?
   b   Why does Jenny think that Lucy should be there?
   c   Did Jenny enjoy the sports day?
   d   Who won the swimming, and how did Alison do?
   e   What does Lucy think that Mark can do well?
   f   Did he win? Why/why not?

2   Read the dialogues again and look at the phrases in italics (they all use *can, could* or *be able to*). Which ones express:

   permission (or lack of) _____

   possibility (or lack of) _____

   ability (or inability) _____

   Which ones refer to:

   the present _____

   the future _____

   the past _____

   How do we express possibility in the future? _____
   Which ones in *Dialogue 2* indicate that someone tried hard? _____
   What do we use to express this? _____

3   Which of the sentences using *can, could* or *be able to* from the dialogue could be expressed using these phrases?
   Is it possible that? _____

   I don't have the ability to _____

   I don't have permission to _____

   He just managed to _____

4 Match the phrases below with those from the dialogue:

		sentence
a	She didn't manage to keep up.	
b	I don't have that much ability.	
c	Mark has the ability to run.	
d	Do I have permission to go?	
e	It's a pity it wasn't possible for you to come.	
f	I don't have the ability to run.	
g	He just managed to come third.	
h	I don't have permission to come.	
i	It will be possible for you to tell me.	
j	You have the ability to swim so well.	
k	Is it possible for you to come?	

B PRACTICE

5 Fill the gaps in these sentences with the correct forms of *can* or *be able to*.

a Excuse me, _____ I leave the class early today?

b He says he _____ come to the party on Saturday because he's too busy.

c When I was a child I _____ swim much faster than I _____ now.

d It was a very difficult exam but I _____ to finish it.

e It's a very long journey – _____ we take the plane?

f I'm not good at languages – I _____ speak French when I left school, and I still _____ now!

g Boss to secretary: I'm afraid you _____ take your lunch early today; there's too much to do.

h If you help me, we _____ finish the job much sooner.

6 Re-write these sentences, using the correct forms of can and be able to.

a Is it possible for us to stay at home tonight?

b I'm afraid I won't give you permission to buy that.

c I don't have the ability to sing now, though I did when I was younger.

d I didn't manage to contact you, however hard I tried.

e If you come to stay it will be possible for us to visit all the sights.

C COMMUNICATION

7 You and your partner work with a group of children. You want to take them on a weekend camping trip this spring, and you want it to be something special. Read your information and then discuss the trip with your partner.

Student A: Discuss when to hold the trip and what to do to make it special. Use the diary top right and

the information.
You can: sing really well, do magic tricks, make lovely desserts, mix good drinks, play football and swim. You can't: cook, play any instruments.

A

APRIL			MAY
6th/7th			4th/5th
		Holiday - for two weeks	
13th/14th	*Simon coming for the weekend*	*Holiday*	11th/12th
20th/21st			18th/19th
27th/28th		*Work. – conference in London*	25th/26th

Student B: Look at the bottom of the page.

D TEST

8 Complete the paragraph below with the correct verbs.

My sister had a very unusual claim to fame: when she was seventeen she became the first girl to play in our town's football team. Rachel was always a tomboy – when she was ten she (**a**) _____ climb trees as well as any boy, but she (**b**) _____ do any of the things girls normally do, she (**c**) _____ sew or knit! When she started in High School at eleven she asked if she (**d**) _____ play football with the boys, and the school agreed. It was very difficult to combine that with everything else but somehow she (**e**) _____ learn very quickly. When the school told her she (**f**) _____ join the school team if she tried hard, she was delighted. Now she's twenty and she (**g**) _____ still play as well as the boys, although she (**h**) _____ always go to the training sessions because she's now studying to be a doctor. She hopes that she (**i**) _____ in future but she knows that she'll have to study very hard and that she (**j**) _____ (not) play as much as she has in the past.

APRIL			MAY
6th/7th			4th/5th
13th/14th		*meal out Sat evening*	11th/12th *Mum's birthday;*
20th/21st *Hi-Fi being delivered Sat morning*			18th/19th
27th/28th *Weekend in Scotland*			25th/26th

B

Student B: make it special. Use the diary and the information below. You can: cook wonderful Mexican food, play classical guitar, sing, do card tricks, play tennis and row very well. You can't: play any other instruments, do magic tricks, make desserts, play football or any other team game.

Discuss when to hold the trip and what to do to

Signs of obligation

Must, mustn't, have to, should, don't have to, shouldn't

A ANALYSIS

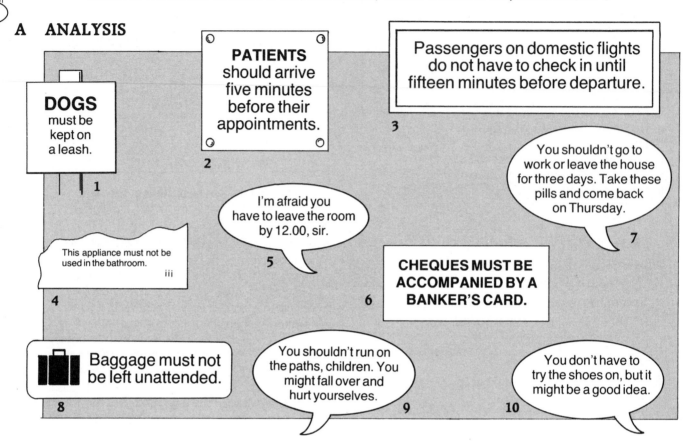

DOGS must be kept on a leash.

1

PATIENTS should arrive five minutes before their appointments.

2

Passengers on domestic flights do not have to check in until fifteen minutes before departure.

3

I'm afraid you have to leave the room by 12.00, sir.

5

You shouldn't go to work or leave the house for three days. Take these pills and come back on Thursday.

7

This appliance must not be used in the bathroom.

iii

4

CHEQUES MUST BE ACCOMPANIED BY A BANKER'S CARD.

6

Baggage must not be left unattended.

8

You shouldn't run on the paths, children. You might fall over and hurt yourselves.

9

You don't have to try the shoes on, but it might be a good idea.

10

B PRACTICE

1 Look at the notices and speech bubbles above. Where might you see or hear these things? Choose from this list:

hotel	airport	shop	park
doctor's surgery		instruction manual	

2 Look at the signs and speech bubbles again and underline the words used to express obligation, necessity and advisability (or lack of).

3 Complete this chart with verbs from exercise 1:

	verbs	examples
obligation to do something (two ways of expressing this)		
obligation not to do something	must not	8
no obligation to do something		
advice to do something		
advice not to do something		

4 Change the sentences below, using the verbs from exercise 3.

a Everyone is obliged to remove their shoes on entry.

_____

b It is advisable for you to take malaria pills but it is essential that you have the typhoid inoculation.

_____
_____

c Is it really necessary for us to book a table at this restaurant?

_____

d We really are obliged not to give you that information.

_____

e It is not advisable for women to wear short skirts in this country.

_____

f Is it necessary for me to pay for the course in advance and would you advise me to buy the books before I start?

_____
_____

5 Make a sentence about each of these signs and notices, using one of the verbs from the notices.

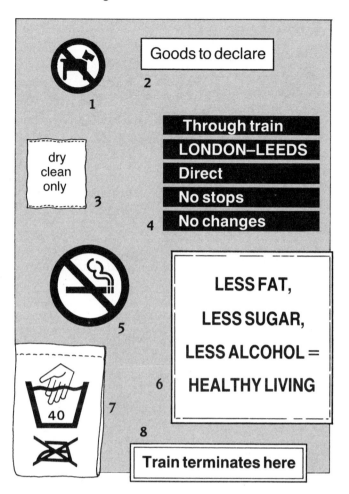

C COMMUNICATION

6 Work in pairs.

Student A: You have recently been youth hostelling. A friend of yours wants to go youth hostelling this summer and he/she is asking you about the rules and regulations. You have a copy of the youth hostel rules to help you give him/her answers (opposite).

Student B: You want to go youth hostelling. A friend of yours has recently been hostelling. Ask him/her about the rules of youth hostelling. You want to find out about the following:

- if you have to book, how much you have to pay and when;
- if it is necessary to be a member of the YHA;
- if you should take your own food and drink;
- if it is best to arrive at a particular time;
- if you have to be in the hostel at a particular time at night;
- if there is anything else you should know.

HOSTEL RULES

1 Payment for the night is required in advance. (1990 – £5.50)

2 Priority is given to members who have booked in advance.

3 Membership cards must be produced on arrival.

4 The hostel is closed between 10.30 and 17.30.

5 The hostel is locked for the night at 22.30, and lights are turned off at 23.00.

6 No smoking is allowed anywhere in the hostel.

7 No alcohol is allowed in the dormitories but wine and beer may be consumed in the dining room.

8 Breakfast and dinner are provided (see the notice for details of times) and a kitchen is available for members who wish to cook their own meals.

9 All hostellers are required to make their beds and keep their rooms clean.

10 Sheet sleeping bags must be used. (For hire @ 50p per night.)

D TEST

7 Fill in the gaps with a suitable verb.

a These days you _____ be rich to buy a computer – they have become so cheap.

b You _____ take an umbrella; it's raining.

c These pills can be dangerous: you _____ take more than the stated dose.

d You _____ have a visa to travel to the United States.

e You _____ let the children play in the street; there are too many cars on the road.

f _____ I take these pills every day, doctor?

g In order to claim the benefit, _____ prove my income?

h You _____ wash this jacket: it will shrink.

i Honestly, I'm quite happy on my own, you _____ come with me.

j She really _____ spend so much on clothes; she can't afford it.

You needn't worry

Mustn't, needn't, don't have to

A ANALYSIS

1 Dr Pam Grimble is a lecturer in law at the university of Mansford. Every Tuesday evening she runs a radio phone-in programme for people who need legal advice.

Read this extract from her programme, answer the questions and complete the government leaflet below.

Pam And our next caller is Tony. So, Tony, what's the problem?

Tony Well, Dr Grimble, I'm living in a rented flat and my landlord phoned me today and asked me to leave tomorrow. You see, I'm really worried because I haven't got anywhere else to go ...

Pam Well, don't worry, Tony, you don't have to leave unless your landlord gets a special document called a 'court order'.

Tony Oh, I see. Do you think I should stop paying the rent now?

Pam No, Tony, you mustn't do that – if you don't pay the rent, the landlord will be able to evict you easily. So you must go on paying it.

Tony Well, what else can I do? Should I get a lawyer?

Pam Oh, you needn't do that. In fact you needn't do anything except wait.

Tony But how can I wait? I'm so worried.

Pam Well, you needn't worry, Tony, you see, the law is on your side. If a landlord wants to evict somebody he has to give at least one month's notice in writing, and then he has to apply for the court order which also takes one month – so you've at least two months to find another flat.

a Is it necessary for Tony to leave tomorrow?
b Is it necessary for Tony to get a lawyer?
c Is it a good idea for Tony to stop paying the rent?

EVICTION PROCEDURES

Landlord's obligations:

1. The landlord must give one month's notice in writing.

2. The landlord _____

Tenant's obligations:

1. The tenant must continue _____

2. The tenant must leave when the court order is received.

---

2 Complete the grammar summary:

	lack of obligation	obligation not to do something
mustn't	[ ]	[ ]
needn't	[ ]	[ ]
don't have to	[ ]	[ ]

What is the difference between *needn't* and *don't have to?*

B PRACTICE

3 Fill the gaps in the sentences with *mustn't* or *needn't*.

a You _____ wear a suit, you can wear anything you like.
b It's quite close, you _____ take the car.
c This vase is very valuable so you _____ break it.
d I don't want Liz to know about her present so you _____ tell her about it.
e Students _____ talk during the exam.
f I'm taking lots of food so you _____ bring any if you don't want to.
g You _____ do that; it's against the rules.
h My father is very strict. He told me I _____ stay out after eleven o'clock.

4 Re-write the sentences in the travel guide using *mustn't* or *don't have to*. Start each sentence with the word 'Tourists'.

REPUBLIC OF RUZANIA

Travel Guide

VISAS
Visas are not required for visits of less than one month.

CURRENCY
Tourists are not allowed to take Ruzanian pesos out of the country.

VACCINATION
Cholera, Typhoid and Yellow Fever vaccinations are recommended although they are not officially required.

DUTY FREE ALLOWANCES
Tourists are allowed to import duty free–goods to the value of US$200 without making a declaration.

SPECIAL RESTRICTIONS
Photography is not permitted within the military zone in the north of Ruzania.
The law forbids the importation of all weapons.

---

a *Visas:* _____

b *Currency:* _____

c *Vaccination:* _____

d *Duty free allowances:* _____

e *Special restrictions:* _____

C   COMMUNICATION

5 Work in pairs.

Student A: You are Dr Grimble (you remember her from Exercise 1). Look at this box. Do not look at your partner's box.
Your partner is going to ask you for some legal advice. Use the information in this government leaflet to answer his/her questions.

LAW FACTSHEET NO. 5

ADVICE FOR PEOPLE BUYING A HOUSE

LEGAL REQUIREMENTS:
- employ a solicitor to complete the legal documents
- do not sign any documents without your solicitor's agreement
- check that the house has building insurance
- do not give the owners a deposit until your solicitor has prepared a contract.

The following suggestions are recommended but are not required by the law:
- employ a surveyor or architect to inspect the house
- do not agree to buy the house until you have arranged to borrow the money from a bank
- make a list of the things you want to buy with the house and give it to your solicitor.

Student B: You have a legal problem and you are going to phone Dr Grimble to ask for advice. Look at this box. Do not look at your partner's box.

You have just seen a house which you want to buy. You've never bought a house before. Here is a list of things you want to ask about:
- legal documents
- borrowing money to pay for the house
- buying the carpets and curtains.
You want to know if these things are necessary:
- house insurance
- paying a deposit to the owners of the house before you buy
- asking an architect or surveyor to inspect the house.

D   TEST

6 Complete the sentences like the example, using *mustn't*, *needn't* or *don't have to*.

People are not allowed to walk on the grass in this park.
You *mustn't walk on the grass in this park*

a   It is not necessary to bring your passport.
You _____

b   The law says that children cannot smoke cigarettes.
Children _____

c   Applicants may bring an example of their work although this is not required.
Applicants _____

d   I know you want to give me a lift but I can easily catch the bus.
You _____

e   Passengers are not permitted to stand during take-off.
Passengers _____

f   Hotel guests are not allowed to smoke in the bedrooms.
Guests _____

g   An umbrella isn't necessary; it isn't going to rain.
You _____

h   Tourists are absolutely forbidden to enter the naval base.
Tourists _____

i   Don't bother to bring me any books. I'm too tired to read.
You _____

j   If you're an experienced swimmer you can miss the class.
Experienced swimmers _____

If I were you ...

First and second conditionals

A ANALYSIS

1 Read the speech bubbles below and put those on the right (numbers 7 to 11) in the correct order to form a dialogue. The ones on the left are in the correct order.

> Now I have Ann on the line. Hello, Ann. What can I do for you?
>
> **1**

> Oh, I've tried. He won't listen. He says I'm selfish. He thinks I should stay in all the time, like him. What will it be like after we're married?
>
> **7**

> Can you tell me why you're worried, Ann?
>
> **2**

> Um, yes. We're saving money, to buy a house. Mick, my boyfriend, stays at home every evening, but I like going out, and if he phones when I'm out, he gets very upset.
>
> **8**

> Does he often phone and find that you're out?
>
> **3**

> Oh, I couldn't do that! If I postponed it, my parents and friends would be really disappointed! Perhaps I should just stay in more; if only I was happy to stay at home, it would be all right.
>
> **9**

> Have you talked to Mick about this? Or is that difficult too?
>
> **4**

> Yes ... and he thinks I should stay in and save my money, but I find that difficult. If I stayed in every night, I'd go mad.
>
> **10**

> Well, Ann, I know you've made arrangements, but if you get married now, you'll have problems, believe me. You need to talk to each other more. If I were you, I'd talk to Mick seriously first. He may not want to, but if he refuses to listen, postpone the wedding for a while.
>
> **5**

> Hello, Tom. Um, I'm engaged to be married. The wedding's in four weeks, but I'm really worried about it.
>
> **11**

> No, it wouldn't be all right! Believe me, Ann, that's not the real problem. If marriages start badly, they go on badly ...
>
> **6**

2 Complete these sentences from the dialogue.

a If he _____ when I'm out, he _____ very upset.

b If I _____ in every night, I _____ mad.

c If you _____ married now, you _____ problems.

d If I _____ you, I _____ to Mick seriously first.

e If he _____ to listen, _____ the wedding for a while.

f If I _____ it, my family and friends _____ really disappointed.

g If only I _____ happy to stay at home, it _____ all right.

h If marriages _____ badly, they _____ badly.

3 Complete the chart by using the sentences from the dialogue. The first row has been done for you.

	sentence number	*present + present*	*present + will*	*past + would*
something: which cannot be true likely to happen unlikely to happen generally true, or which often happens	d, g			✓

There is something different about sentence **e**. What? Why?

B PRACTICE

4 Complete the sentences about these pictures.

a If you _____ water to 100°C, it
_____ .

b You _____ if you _____ too much.

c If you _____ plants, they
_____ .

d You _____ fit if you _____ exercise.

e She _____ if she _____ more money.

f If he _____ now, he _____ .

5 Match the clauses below to make sensible pieces of advice.

a If you really wanted more friends,
b If you don't tell him you're not coming,
c If you were in my situation,
d If you put a cat and a dog together,
e If you don't like the colour,
f If you cancelled your dates in advance,

1 you'd do the same.
2 I'll change it.
3 they fight.
4 you'd join a club.
5 she'd be happier.
6 he'll be very upset.

C COMMUNICATION

6 In pairs, answer the questions below, using the correct conditional.

a What do you do if a shop assistant gives you too much change?
_____

b What would you do if you heard screams late at night?
_____

c What do you do if you see money lying on the ground?
_____

d What would you do if you saw your best friend's wife/husband with another man/woman?
_____

e What do you do if you make a serious mistake at school/work?
_____

f What would you do if you saw someone attack another person in the street?
_____

Now join with another pair, to make groups of four. Compare your answers, and justify them if they are different. Can you write any questions of your own?

D TEST

7 Complete the sentences by using the verbs below in the correct tense.

arrive	be (x2)	become	faint
feel	find	forget	go (x2)	grow
have	ignore	pay	phone
put	resign	speak (x2)	wear

a If the weather _____ good tomorrow, we _____ to the beach.

b Look at those shoes! I _____ high heels if I _____ that tall.

c Kate and Andy are always late. If they actually _____ at the party on time, everyone _____ with shock.

d Everyone knows that most plants _____ better if you _____ them in sunlight.

e If people _____ rudely to me, I _____ them.

f If my boss _____ to me like that again, I _____ from the job.

g Jane's not suited to teaching. She _____ it easier to deal with those children if she _____ more patience.

h It's a well-known fact that animals _____ aggressive if they _____ threatened.

i She always remembers to visit her grandmother on Thursdays. If she _____ to go one week, she _____ on the Friday.

j Our landlord never leaves us alone. If we _____ the rent on time, he _____ us every five minutes!

If you hadn't ...

Third conditional

A ANALYSIS

1 Complete the sentences with one of the verbs below, then put them into order according to the pictures.

| brake   ask   tread   rush   drop   hit   shout |

a Sally ran into the kitchen and _____ on a piece of glass. □□
b She _____ him to do the washing up. □□
c Sally saw a cat run across the road and _____ at Fred to stop. □
d One day Fred was sleeping when his wife woke him up. □
e Her foot was badly cut so Fred _____ her to the hospital. □
f As he was washing up he _____ a glass and it broke. □
g He _____ hard and the car behind _____ them. □
h Fred broke several bones and had to stay in hospital. □

2 Look at Sally's words in the last picture and decide whether the statements below are true (T) or false (F).

a Fred braked hard. [ ]
b Fred didn't brake hard. [ ]
c They had an accident. [ ]
d They didn't have an accident. [ ]

3 Look at the four sentences below and complete the chart.

A If John had come, it would have been a good party.
B If John had come, it wouldn't have been a good party.
C If John hadn't come, it would have been a good party.
D If John hadn't come, it wouldn't have been a good party.

true facts	A	B	C	D
John came.				
John didn't come.				
It was a good party.				
It wasn't a good party.				

B   PRACTICE

4 Complete this dialogue between Fred and Sally. (Use the verbs in exercise 1.)

Sally Well, if you _____ so hard, we _____ the accident.

Fred If you _____ at me, I _____ so hard.

Sally If you _____ so much, I _____ at you.

Fred If you _____ on the glass, I _____ to the hospital.

Sally But if you _____ the glass, I _____ on it!

Fred And if you _____ me to do the washing up, I _____ the glass!

Sally So, it's all my fault, is it?

Fred Yes, if you _____ me to do the washing up, we _____ the accident!

5 These sentences are all about the past. Change them to speculate about the past, using the third conditional.

a I had a car accident last year because I was tired. If I hadn't been tired, _____

b My friend almost skied into a tree last year, but he saw it in time.

_____

c I didn't see the broken glass on the ground, so I trod on it.

_____

d I didn't shout because I didn't see the cat.

_____

e The ambulance came very quickly and saved my life.

_____

f I didn't have any insurance for my mountaineering holiday, so I had to pay the doctor's bills.

_____

C   COMMUNICATION

6 Work in pairs and look at one picture each. Think about the period the picture shows, and think of everyday life in that period, for example, what did people eat/wear, where did they live, how did they travel, and so on. Ask your partner about his/her picture, like this:

If you had lived in the Middle Ages/Stone Age, what would you have eaten/drunk/worn?

Then answer your partner's questions, for example:

If I'd lived in the Middle Ages/Stone Age, I'd have eaten raw meat/drunk wine etc.

Use your imagination to make your answers interesting!

D   TEST

7 Complete the gaps, using the third conditional.

a I _____ so angry if he _____ me. (be, kick)

b If we _____ in the 1920s, we _____ the Charleston. (live, dance)

c _____ they _____ you if you _____ the letter? (visit, send)

d She _____ the job if you _____ her such a bad reference! (get, give)

e If I _____ that competition, I _____ a new car. (win, buy)

What if ...?

Mixed conditionals

A   ANALYSIS

1   The Beaton family are on a driving holiday in the South of France. Their car has just broken down. Look at the picture, read the sentences and write the characters' names.

a 'The car wouldn't break down so often if Dad was a better mechanic!' _____

b 'If we hadn't broken down we would be in St Tropez by now!' _____

c 'If I'd bought a better car we wouldn't have broken down!' _____

d 'If I phone the local garage they'll send a mechanic to fix the car.' _____

2   Look at the example sentences above. Are these statements true (T) or false (F)?

a (i)   The car breaks down quite often.   [   ]
     (ii) Dad is a good mechanic.   [   ]
     (iii) Dad used to be a good mechanic.   [   ]

b (i)   The car hasn't broken down.   [   ]
     (ii) The family is now in St Tropez.   [   ]

c (i)   Mr Beaton didn't buy a very good car.   [   ]
     (ii) Mr Beaton bought a Rolls Royce.   [   ]

d (i)   Steve thinks a mechanic will come if he phones the garage.   [   ]

3   The phrases in exercise 1 are all examples of conditional sentences. Match the grammar summaries below with the example sentences in exercise 1 above, and with the correct functions from the list below:

a Type 1
    if + present tense + will + infinitive
    Example: _____   Function: _____

b Type 2
    if + simple past + would + infinitive
    Example: _____   Function: _____

c Type 3
    if + past perfect + would + perfect infinitive
    Example: _____   Function: _____

d Mixed
    if + past perfect + would + infinitive
    Example: _____   Function: _____

Functions:

A – to talk about an unlikely or unreal condition (present or future time)

B – to talk about an unreal condition in the past

C – to talk about an unreal condition in the past with an unreal result in the present

D – to talk about a probable condition

B PRACTICE

4 Put the verbs in brackets into the correct form.

a If Hilary arrives late she (miss) _____ the start of the film.

b I wouldn't marry him if he (be) _____ the last man on earth!

c If she (take) _____ the next flight she would be there on time.

d The car will overheat if you (drive) _____ it too fast.

e If Mike goes to Paris this weekend, he (leave) _____ the dog at the kennels.

f I'd go to the theatre every night if I (live) _____ in London.

g Henry will never improve if he (not practise) _____ .

h If I had a million dollars I (spend) _____ it all on ice-cream.

5 Look at the situation and write a sentence.
Example:
You are cold because you didn't bring a jacket.
If I'd brought a jacket I wouldn't be cold now.
Susan failed the exam because she didn't revise.
If Susan had revised she wouldn't have failed the exam.

a Peter is lost because he didn't bring a map.

_____

b I'm embarrassed because I forgot to bring my wallet.

_____

c Sam was late because he missed the bus.

_____

d Juan is in hospital because he fell off his motorbike.

_____

e Lady Diana became famous because she married Prince Charles.

_____

f Emma went to prison because she didn't pay her tax bill.

_____

C COMMUNICATION

6 Work in pairs.
'What if ...?'
Complete the sentence:
If Thomas Edison hadn't been born, ...

Now match these 'if' clauses with the results:

1 If Christopher Columbus hadn't discovered America, ...

2 If people's noses grew longer every time they told a lie, ...

3 If Alexander Graham Bell hadn't been born, ...

4 If Sigmund Freud had had a happy childhood, ...

5 If Galileo hadn't bought a telescope, ...

A ... we would still be sending messages by pigeon.

B ... Neil Armstrong would never have stepped on the moon.

C ... there wouldn't be any hamburger restaurants.

D ... a lot of psychiatrists would be bankrupt.

E ... politicians would need big handkerchiefs.

7 Now look at this sequence of conditionals:

If the motor car hadn't been invented, _____

If the motor car hadn't been invented, *we would have to walk.*

If we had to walk, _____

If we had to walk, we would all be healthy.

If we were healthy, _____

If we were healthy, we would live longer.

If we lived longer, _____

Work in groups. Each student must continue the sequence like the example above. See how long you can keep going!

Start with this condition:

If human beings were the size of ants, _____

D TEST

8 Put the verbs in brackets into the correct form.

a If I'd passed those exams I (be) _____ a doctor now.

b If you look in the cupboard you (find) _____ the coffee.

c I wouldn't have come if I (know) _____ about the entrance fee.

d If I (win) _____ the competition I'll buy a new house.

e If Sam (bring) _____ his map we wouldn't have got lost.

f Jane will only play Juliet if you (play) _____ Romeo.

g If I (have) _____ a garden I'd spend all my time there.

h I wouldn't be so lonely now if I (make) _____ more friends when I was younger.

i Helga (be) _____ much happier if she lived in a warmer climate.

j The car wouldn't have broken down if Mr Beaton (remember) _____ to check the oil and water.

Holiday experiences
Verbs followed by infinitive or -ing

A ANALYSIS

This year the Turnbull family felt like taking a holiday together and their grandparents agreed to come with them. Grandpa suggested going to a hot country, so they decided to visit the Mediterranean where they could enjoy relaxing by the beach and attempt to get suntanned. They carefully avoided taking their holiday in the high season because they dislike sitting on crowded beaches. Sally is learning to speak Greek so they chose to go to Greece.

Jim was swimming a few minutes ago but now he has stopped to have an ice-cream. Sally stopped swimming last month because she broke her leg. Mum remembered to bring the sun cream but she has forgotten to bring her sunglasses. Dad is trying to open a bottle. He has forgotten leaving the corkscrew in the hotel this morning. Grandma tried swimming in the sea this morning but the water was too cold. Grandpa is looking for his glasses: he doesn't remember putting them in his shirt pocket at breakfast.

1 There are fourteen verbs in the passages above which are followed by the infinitive or *-ing* form. Find the verbs and put them into the correct column in this chart. Some have already been done for you.

verbs followed by:

A *infinitive*	B *-ing*	C *infinitive or -ing* depending on meaning
decide	feel like	stop

2 Look carefully at the use of the verbs in column C. Using the infinitive or *-ing* after the verbs depends on the meaning. Complete this chart by matching the meanings with *-ing* or the infinitive:

	-ing	infinitive
a stop		
• to stop an action	[ ]	[ ]
• to stop in order to do something else	[ ]	[ ]
b remember		
• recall something from the past	[ ]	[ ]
• remember to do something you might easily forget	[ ]	[ ]

	-ing	infinitive
c forget		
• look back at something you didn't do in the past	[ ]	[ ]
• think about something you did in the past although you can't remember it	[ ]	[ ]
d try		
• make an effort to do something difficult	[ ]	[ ]
• do something as an experiment or test	[ ]	[ ]

B PRACTICE

3 Complete these sentences with the correct form of the verb in brackets:

a Most people enjoy (watch) _____ television.
b I really must learn (drive) _____ soon.
c Last year we decided (go) _____ to Florida.
d My father agreed (pay) _____ for my guitar.
e I don't feel like (go out) _____ this evening.
f Clare dislikes (live) _____ with her parents.
g I suggested (put) _____ the money in a bank.
h I try to avoid (argue) _____ with my girlfriend.

4 Complete the dialogue with the correct forms of the verbs in brackets.

Anna and Pete are about to leave on their summer holiday.

Anna Did you remember (**a**) (pack) _____ the beach towels?

Pete Sorry, I forgot (**b**) (do) _____ that. Look, they're here on the kitchen table.

Anna Okay, my bag's pretty full but I'll try (**c**) (put) _____ them in it.

Pete Oh, I really dislike (**d**) (pack) _____. It's so boring!

Anna Never mind, it's all worth it. Do you remember (**e**) (go) _____ to India last year?

Pete Of course, I'll certainly never forget (**f**) (have) _____ all those injections. And I'm glad I tried (**g**) (eat) _____ all that spicy Indian food – it was delicious.

Anna Yes, I remember. In fact you didn't stop (**h**) (eat) _____ throughout the time we were there!

Pete We had some strange experiences, didn't we? Do you remember the time we were driving around Delhi and you stopped (**i**) (give) _____ money to a blind man?

Anna Oh yes, within thirty seconds we were surrounded by beggars!

Pete It was a great holiday but I'm glad we decided (**j**) (go) _____ to Spain this year.

C COMMUNICATION

5 Work in pairs.
Your partner has decided to join the Friendship Agency. Interview your partner and complete the questionnaire.

The Friendship Agency

Do you find it difficult to meet new people and make friends – friends who share your interests and experiences?

Don't be a stay-at-home! Join our agency and you could be going to parties every night! Call us free on 0009 76 76 76 now!

The Friendship Agency

PERSONALITY QUESTIONNAIRE
Name: _____
Age: _____ Sex: _____
Please answer these questions as honestly as you can so that we can help you find friends you will really like:

_____

1. What is the most embarrassing thing you can remember doing?
_____

2. What is the most difficult thing you have ever tried to do?
_____

3. What is the most stupid thing you have ever forgotten to do?
_____

4. What sort of things do you usually feel like doing in the evenings?
_____

5. What sort of person do you usually avoid meeting?
_____

6. What sort of person do you usually choose to be friendly with?
_____

7. What do you enjoy doing at the weekends?
_____

When you have completed the questionnaire, divide into small groups. (Your partner should join a different group.) Now compare your questionnaires. Can you find any suitable friends for your partner?

D TEST

6 Choose the correct verb form to fill the gaps in these sentences:

a I've decided _____ to university when I finish school.
(i) going   (ii) to go

b I know it's not easy, but try _____ your best in the exam.
(i) doing   (ii) to do

c This job is exhausting. I'm going to stop _____ a rest.
(i) having   (ii) to have

d When I was a child I remember _____ horses in the street.
(i) seeing   (ii) to see

e My secretary isn't very reliable. She often forgets _____ the files in the correct order.
(i) to put   (ii) putting

f That athlete is attempting _____ the world record.
(i) to break   (ii) breaking

g My doctor has told me to stop _____
(i) to smoke   (ii) smoking

h Sometimes students can't avoid _____ mistakes.
(i) to make   (ii) making

i I wanted to go swimming and Sarah agreed _____ with me.
(i) to come   (ii) coming

j Gerry suggested _____ a holiday in Florida.
(i) to take   (ii) taking

Eyewitness!

Verbs of perception with the present participle/infinitive

A ANALYSIS

In late December, 1973, the volcano overshadowing the fishing port of Heimaey, Westmann Islands (Iceland), erupted. Fortunately, the presence of the fishing fleet in the port meant that the town was evacuated without loss of life.

1 Read the account of Arne, an eyewitness, and complete the sentences on the right.

'I was out that evening with a friend, just having a walk down by the port. We suddenly felt the ground shake, just once. We thought we'd imagined it, but then it happened again. Then we heard the volcano roar. We looked up, and at that moment we saw a column of flame shoot out into the black night sky; it was amazing. It all happened within about three minutes. Then we ran home; by this time we could hear people all around us shouting to each other "Go to the port". My family and I collected a few things and ran to the port, where we stood and waited for a boat. As we waited a feeling of panic started to grow; it was almost as if we could smell and feel the boiling lava approaching. Finally we got on a boat, and from the deck we watched the lava flowing slowly into the outskirts of the town and we listened to it crushing the few houses in its path. It was several months before we came back, but I'll never forget what I saw that night.'

a On the evening of the eruption the two friends were _____
b First they felt _____
c Then they heard _____ and they saw _____
d They _____, collected _____ and they_____.
e At the port they thought they could feel and smell _____
f On the boat they watched _____ and they listened to _____.

2 Look at these six verbs from the passage:

| see | hear | watch | listen to | feel | smell |

What do they have in common?
Write below the verbs which follow them in the passage, exactly as they appear:
feel   + (1) shake   (2) _____
hear   + (1) _____ (2) _____
watch   + _____   see + _____
smell   + _____   listen to + _____

3 Complete the chart below with ticks according to whether the *-ing* form or the infinitive follows the verb.

	-ing	infinitive
a We felt the ground shake.		
b We heard the volcano roar.		
c We saw a column of flame shoot out.		
d We could hear people shouting.		
e We could smell and feel the lava approaching.		
f We watched the lava flowing.		
g We listened to the lava crushing the few houses in its path.		

Now look at these time lines which illustrate two of the verbs:

We felt the ground shake.

the ground shook
we felt it

We watched the lava flowing slowly ...

the lava was flowing
we watched it

In the first case, we experience the complete action and usually the action is very short. In the second, the action starts before we are aware of it, and we experience only part of it.

Do we use the infinitive of the verb to show we have experienced all of the action or only part of it?

B PRACTICE

4 Complete the sentences with the correct form of the verbs in brackets.

a She was listening to her daughter (practise) _____ at the piano.

b The judges observed the gymnasts (do) _____ their exercises only for about five minutes.

c I heard the glass in the window (shatter) _____ as the man put his fist through it.

d We watched the children (play) _____ football this afternoon.

e The motorist obviously noticed the old man (fall over) _____ but he just drove past him.

f We were all getting really hungry as we could smell the food (cook) _____ .

g I saw the girl (drop) _____ the letter so I picked it up for her.

h Despite the anaesthetic I felt the dentist's drill (hit) _____ my nerve.

5 Complete this eyewitness account of an explosion using suitable verbs in the correct form.

A What exactly did you hear?

B Well, first I heard the bomb (**a**) _____ and then I heard the glass in the car windows (**b**) _____ .

A Did you see anything?

B Yes, first I noticed someone (**c**) _____ from the car then I saw the car windows (**d**) _____ , and I could smell metal and plastic (**e**) _____ .

A And then?

B I called the police, of course, then I went back to the scene, where I watched people (**f**) _____ around the car.

A What happened afterwards?

B I made a statement to the police and listened to other people (**g**) _____ their statements. It was really strange later on listening to myself (**h**) _____ on the news!

C COMMUNICATION

6 Look at the poster advertising a new film with 'Sensurround', a technique where you experience the film with all your senses; those of smell and feeling as well as sight and hearing.

Student A: You want to see the film. Your partner has already seen it. Ask him/her about the film and remember to ask about the special effects, e.g. what you can hear/see/feel/smell.

Student B: You have just been to see the film in the poster above. Make notes about what you saw/ heard/felt/smelt and tell your partner all about it, for example, *There was a fire on the spaceship and we could smell the plastic burning!*

D TEST

7 Complete each of the sentences below with a suitable verb of perception and the correct form of the verb in brackets.

a She wasn't in the room but she _____ him (crack) _____ his head on the floor as he fell.

b I can _____ something (burn) _____ . Have you left the cooker on?

c I think these shoes are too tight. I can _____ my toes (tingle) _____ .

d Didn't you _____ the car (hit) _____ the wall? You were standing right in front of it!

e A violinist lives upstairs. I have to _____ him (practise) _____ every evening for hours.

Christmas presents

Verbs with two objects

A ANALYSIS

1 The Johnson family love Christmas because they all enjoy giving and receiving presents.
Study this chart and complete the sentences below:

AUNT ELIZABETH → [bicycle] → STEVEN

UNCLE BILL → [watch] → TERESA

STEVEN → [box of chocolates] → AUNT SARAH

HARRY → [perfume] → SYLVIA

a Aunt Elizabeth gave _____ a bicycle.
b Uncle Bill gave _____ to Teresa.
c _____ gave _____ a box of chocolates.
d Harry gave _____ to _____.

Now match each of the sentences above with one of these patterns:

A *subject + verb + direct object + preposition + indirect object*
B *subject + verb + indirect object + direct object*

What does the indirect object usually refer to?

2 These verbs are sometimes used in the passive. Complete these sentences from the chart.

a A bicycle was given to _____ by Aunt Elizabeth.
b Teresa was given _____ by _____.
c _____ was given to Aunt Sarah by _____.
d _____ was given to _____ by Harry.

What two patterns do these sentences follow?

3 Some verbs can only follow one pattern. Look at these examples:
Aunt Elizabeth explained the instructions to Steven.
Uncle Bill described the watch to Teresa.
Harry suggested a box of chocolates to Steven.
What are the three verbs?
Which pattern do they follow?

B PRACTICE

4 These sentences refer to the chart in exercise 1. Each sentence is incorrect. Find the mistake and write the corrected version underneath.

a Aunt Elizabeth was given a bicycle by Steven.

b Sylvia bought Harry some perfume.

c Steven gave to Aunt Sarah a box of chocolates.

d A watch was given to Uncle Bill by Teresa.

e Aunt Sarah bought a box of chocolates for Steven.

f Harry was sent some perfume by Sylvia.

5 Re-write these sentences beginning with the words given.

Example:
Carrie was sent a bunch of flowers by Charles.
Charles *sent Carrie a bunch of flowers.*

a Mrs Jackson offered me a cup of tea.
I _____

b This house was left to me by my grandfather.
My grandfather_____.

c You've been brought a parcel by the postman.
The postman _____.

d The manager paid her fifty dollars.
She _____.

e The operating instructions were explained to me by Tom.
Tom _____.

f The house designs have been described to me by the architect.
The architect _____.

C COMMUNICATION

6 The Armstrong family live in a remote village in Scotland, but most of their relatives live a long way away – in England or in other countries. At Christmas all their relatives send them Christmas presents. The Armstrongs have a kitten that loves chewing things and, unfortunately, she ate the labels on some of the presents around the Christmas tree. Mrs Armstrong had to open the presents.
Can you help Mrs Armstrong? Work in pairs. Use this information to decide who each present is for, and who sent them.

The Armstrong family
Mrs Armstrong loves decorating her home.
Mr Armstrong is a businessman.
Amanda loves going to parties.
Carol is a student.
Mike's favourite subject is mathematics.
Philip is always late!

The family relatives
Aunt Mimi works in a bookshop in Glasgow.
Uncle Clive has retired and lives in Switzerland.
Uncle Stephen is a diplomat in Istanbul.
Aunt Harriet works for a Japanese electronics company in Cardiff.
Uncle Henry is a fashion designer in London.
Aunt Mary is an English teacher in Madrid.

D TEST

7 There is a preposition missing from some of these sentences. Decide which sentences have a missing preposition and, if necessary, re-write the sentences with a suitable preposition in the correct place.

a Hilary described her new dress me.
_____

b Paul sent his wife a bouquet of red roses.
_____

c My daughter was taken the hospital by the ambulance.
_____

d The Highway Code was explained me by my driving instructor.
_____

e Mrs Graham doesn't give her children presents.
_____

f A 10% bonus was given to Michael his boss.
_____

g Patrick described the new design Helen.
_____

h Ann was given a ring by her boyfriend.
_____

i The guide suggested the Ritz Hotel the rich tourists.
_____

j Lady Melton paid her maid £5 an hour.
_____

Partners

Stative and dynamic verbs

A ANALYSIS

1 John is sitting in the park. He is eating an ice-cream which tastes delicious and he is thinking about his girlfriend, Judy. He thinks she is beautiful. He loves her very much and he knows that she wants to marry him. He feels she would be a perfect wife.

John is feeling happy. The air smells clean and fresh. He hears the birds singing and sees the flowers amongst the trees. He wishes Judy was with him. Judy also likes parks. But Judy is living in the centre of the city. She owns a small flat which is a long way from the park. She dislikes living there but it is very convenient for her office.

Some verbs are usually not used in the continuous tenses. Read the passage and decide which of the verbs below are not normally used in the continuous tenses, then tick the box (some of them have been done already):

A _____

own	[ ]
belong to	[✓]
have (possession)	[✓]

B _____

know	[ ]
understand	[✓]
believe	[✓]
think (mental activity)	[ ]

C _____

love	[ ]
hate	[✓]
like	[ ]
dislike	[ ]
prefer	[✓]
think (have an opinion)	[ ]
feel (have an opinion)	[ ]
feel (describing emotion)	[ ]
wish	[ ]

D _____

see	[ ]
hear	[ ]
smell (state)	[ ]
smell (action)	[ ]
taste (state)	[ ]
taste (action)	[ ]
feel (state)	[ ]
feel (action)	[ ]

2 Now match each of the sets of verbs with one of these categories and write the name of the category on the appropriate line.

Verbs of opinion and emotion ___
Verbs of possession ___
Verbs of the senses ___
Verbs describing state of mind ___

3 Look at the verbs of the senses. Can you make any general rule about when these verbs are not used in the continuous tenses?

B PRACTICE

4 Match the subject, the object and the correct verb form to make ten sentences. The first one has been done for you:

subject	*verb*	*object*
a This pudding	is thinking	that English is difficult.
b Some students	is feeling	in God.
c Those dirty socks	believe	delicious.
d Patrizio	hear	unhappy.
e The cook	feels	about his girlfriend.
f Many people	smell	uncomfortable.
g The boutique owners	is tasting	the birds singing.
h Carmen	think	the new perfume.
i This old bed	tastes	his new garlic sauce.
j People who get up early	are smelling	disgusting!

5 Complete the mini dialogues by putting the verb in brackets into the correct tense.

a Are you enjoying the meal?
Yes, it (taste) _____ delicious.
b Who's living in the big house?
Lord Emsley, it (belong to) _____ him.
c What's Claire doing?
She (smell) _____ the roses.
d Are you enjoying London?
Oh yes, I (love) _____ it.
e You look worried.
Yes, I (think) _____ about the exam tomorrow.
f How is Ellen coping in New York?
Fine, she (know) _____ the city quite well now.
g What on earth is the chef doing?
He (taste) _____ the soup.
h What an awful perfume!
Yuk, it (smell) _____ terrible!
i Do you like the pullover, madam?
Oh, yes, it (feel) _____ beautifully soft.
j Oh dear, the guide's speaking in Italian.
That's no problem, I (understand) _____ Italian quite well.

C COMMUNICATION

6 !!FIND A PARTNER!!
You work for a dating agency. Your job is to find a suitable partner for each of your clients.

Instructions:
Complete the information on each of the client record cards, using your imagination!

When you have finished, go around the class and try to match your clients with suitable partners by asking questions about the other students' clients.

NAME: _____ AGE: _____
OCCUPATION: _____
LIKES: _____
DISLIKES: _____
OPINIONS: _____
AMBITIONS: _____

NAME: _____ AGE: ___
OCCUPATION: _____
LIKES: _____
DISLIKES: _____
OPINIONS: _____
AMBITIONS: _____

D TEST

7 Do you remember John from exercise 1? This is John's girlfriend, Judy:

Complete the passage by putting the verbs in brackets into the correct tense:

Judy is sitting at her typewriter. She isn't working; she (**a**) (think) _____ about her boyfriends. She (**b**) (hate) _____ her job almost as much as she (**c**) (dislike) _____ John. He is so silly, he's always walking in the park, (**d**) (smell) _____ the flowers and thinking about nature. Judy (**e**) (prefer) _____ Ramon. Ramon is Spanish and he is very rich. He (**f**) (have) _____ an apartment in Barcelona but he is living in a flat near Judy at the moment. He (**g**) (belong to) _____ all the best nightclubs and he (**h**) (know) _____ lots of famous people. Judy (**i**) (believe) _____ Ramon will marry her one day, but Judy (**j**) (not know) _____ that Ramon is returning to Barcelona next month.

Look it up!

Phrasal verbs

A   ANALYSIS

1 Read the telephone conversation and decide whether the statements are true (T) or false (F).

Anne   Have you spoken to Jimmy?

Mark   Yes, *I rang him up* this morning.

Anne   How are the arrangements for the party going?

Mark   Fine, he's *set up a disco* in the back garden.

Anne   That'll be noisy, I hope the neighbours don't complain!

Mark   Well, he can always *turn the volume down* if they do.

Anne   So everything's ready for six o'clock...

Mark   No, I forgot to tell you, the party has been *put back* to eight o'clock.

Anne   Why's that?

Mark   Because Jimmy's parents aren't *bringing the food over* until then.

Anne   Why don't you invite that girl you met last week? Have you got her telephone number?

Mark   Yes, *I looked up the number* in the telephone directory. I only hope she doesn't *turn me down!*

a   Mark visited Jimmy this morning.   [   ]
b   Jimmy will stop the disco if the neighbours complain.   [   ]
c   The party will be starting later than originally planned.   [   ]
d   There won't be any food at the party.   [   ]
e   Mark hopes that the girl will agree to come to the party.   [   ]

Which phrasal verbs in the dialogue have these meanings?
1   to reduce sound
2   to refuse an invitation
3   to bring something to a particular place
4   to telephone someone
5   to change something to a later time
6   to organise/arrange something
7   to find information in a book

2 Study the phrases in italics in the telephone dialogue. Try to find examples of each of the following patterns (the first one has been done for you) and then answer the questions underneath.

verb + pronoun + particle

rang   him   up

_____

verb + particle + pronoun

_____

_____

verb + noun object + particle

_____

_____

verb + particle + noun object

_____

_____

a   Which pattern is not possible with phrasal verbs?
b   Can you find an example of a phrasal verb in the passive form in the dialogue? What pattern does it follow?

B PRACTICE

3 Re-write these sentences by replacing the verb and noun object with a phrasal verb and pronoun. The first part of the phrasal verb is written in brackets.
Example:
James rejected the job offer (turn ...)
James turned it down.

a Why don't you find the word in the dictionary? (look ...)

_____

b Hilary will telephone Amanda this afternoon. (ring ...)

_____

c That radio's too loud. Please reduce the sound. (turn ...)

_____

d Can you change the appointment to a later time? (put ...)

_____

e Ali is organising the exhibition in the lobby. (set ...)

_____

f We erected the tent in a field. (put ...)

_____

g Why don't you suggest that idea to the committee? (put ...)

_____

h Don't forget to return the books tomorrow. (bring ...)

_____

4 Complete these sentences by filling in the gaps with these words:

on up set turned turn put up brought off up

a Cadillac have _____ the launch of the new model back by two months because the new factory hasn't been put _____ yet.
b My cousin _____ his new computer over to my house but unfortunately we couldn't find out how to turn it _____.
c I would really like to take _____ painting as a new hobby and I want to _____ up the spare bedroom as a studio.
d When the government _____ down their demands the terrorists tried to blow _____ a police station.
e My neighbour got so angry when I refused to _____ down the volume on my stereo that she turned _____ the electricity to my flat!

C GAME

5 Work with a partner. Find all the synonyms hidden in the word square and match them with the phrasal verbs on the left. The first one has been done for you. The first pair to complete the exercise is the winner!

```
C A N C E L L V T D
R S G E X P L O D E
E B I O T U P W E L
T D E L I V E R M A
U C M X N Y E S P Y
R S U G G E S T L Q
N P X M U V A A O Z
C R D P I O N R Y M
R E F U S E L T W Q
J D W P H O N E A Z
```

put out
extinguish _____

call off _____

bring over _____

ring up _____

bring back _____

put off _____	put forward _____
take on _____	blow up _____
take up _____	turn down _____

D TEST

6 Complete the answers to these questions using a suitable pronoun with a phrasal verb from the list below.

put out	ring up	put off
turn down	bring over	bring back
call off	blow up	turn down	look up

a Did you read about what the terrorists did to that plane?
Yes, they _____ in mid air.
b Do you really need to have that radio on so loud?
Okay, I'll _____ if you like.
c Have you telephoned your parents yet?
Yes, I _____ yesterday.
d Are you taking your driving test tomorrow?
No, I've _____ until next month.
e What's the meaning of 'osteopathy'?
I don't know, I'll _____ in the dictionary.
f Has your sister returned your umbrella?
Yes, she _____ this morning.
g Did your boss accept that financial report?
I'm afraid not, she's _____.
h Did anyone bring the glasses?
Yes, Michiko _____ this morning.
i Is that building still on fire?
No, the firemen managed _____ about ten minutes ago.
j Are you going to see the game today?
No, they've _____ because of the bad weather.

English is spoken here

Passives

A ANALYSIS

1 Look at the phrases above.
  a Where would you expect to find these?
  b What is different about **D**?

2 All the phrases use the passive form. Study this list of reasons for using the passive and decide if they apply to any of the phrases in exercise 1:
  ● the cause of the action is not known.
  ● the action is more interesting/important than the cause.
  ● we want to put the most interesting/important information at the beginning of the sentence.
  ● it's not necessary to describe the cause because we know it already.

3 Here are some notices. Decide whether these notices would be improved by using the passive form and whether the agent should be included. Then re-write the sentences like the example.

People who wear this garment must wash it in cold water only.
This garment must be washed in cold water only.

  a We apologise that the operations manager has cancelled flight KL167 because of weather conditions.
  _____

  b Passengers can obtain refunds from the ticket office.
  _____

  c The waiters will serve drinks in the hotel lounge at six o'clock.
  _____

  d The staff in this shop accept payment by Eurocheque.
  _____

  e The director filmed this movie on location in Ireland.
  _____

Using the verbs from the sentences above and in exercise 1, complete the gaps in this chart:

	Active	Passive
present simple	accept	is accepted
	speaks	_____
past simple	filmed	_____
	_____	was recorded
present perfect	_____	has been cancelled
	have delayed	_____
modal verbs	must wash	_____
	_____	can be obtained
	will serve	_____
	_____	must not be dry-cleaned
	_____	should be refrigerated

B PRACTICE

4 Complete the gaps by using a verb from the list. Remember to use the passive form of the correct tense.

> wash   pay   win   accept   rob   clean
> not invade   discover   deliver   teach

  a The bank _____ last night.
  b Travellers cheques _____ in this store.
  c This pullover should _____ by hand.
  d Your new car _____ tomorrow.
  e The first prize _____ by a man from Manchester.
  f Penicillin _____ by Alexander Fleming.
  g Britain _____ since the year 1066.
  h This account must _____ within 28 days.
  i The hotel rooms _____ every day.
  j Next week your class _____ by Mrs Girton.

5 Re-write these sentences like the example:
This meal should be defrosted by purchasers before heating.
Purchasers should defrost this meal before heating.

a Breakfast is served between 8 and 10 a.m. at this hotel.

_____

b A cure for cancer has been discovered by scientists at last!

_____

c The monkeys will be fed by the zoo keepers at four o'clock.

_____

d The computer was installed by the engineer two months ago.

_____

e This shirt can be washed by you at any temperature.

_____

C GAME

6 The Sentence Jigsaw
Work in teams of three. Your task is to combine the words you are given to complete the chart of thirteen passive sentences. You must put the verbs into the correct passive form. The first team to fill the chart with thirteen correct sentences is the winner!

Student A: Look at the chart below. Your job is to read out the words in the chart, ask your team mates to help you complete the sentences, and then write them in:

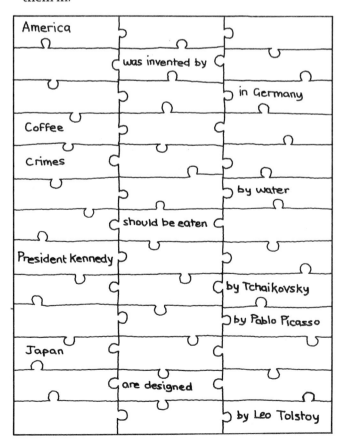

Student B: Cover the chart with a piece of paper and look at Box B.

Box B:

	radio
to compose	to export
islands	most buildings
the 1812 Overture	in Dallas
to manufacture	to discover
Chinese food	by an Emperor
to investigate	Marconi

Student C: Turn the page upside down and look at Box C at the bottom.

D TEST

7 Complete each sentence so that it means the same as the sentence above it.

Example:
People shouldn't take children on long journeys.
Children shouldn't be taken on long journeys.

a You may take photographs in this museum.
Photographs _____

b Somebody has lost the keys.
The keys _____

c Sherlock Holmes investigated many famous crimes.
_____ by Sherlock Holmes.

d Doctors have discovered a cure for the common cold!
A cure for the common cold _____

e The postal service will send on your letters to the new address.
Your letters _____

f They change the sheets every week.
The sheets _____

g People eat a lot of hamburgers in the United States.
A lot of hamburgers _____

h You must not bring dogs into this park.
Dogs _____

i The Italians have designed the best outfits this season.
The best outfits this season _____
by the Italians.

j Factory workers manufactured this TV in Korea.
This TV _____

Box C:

by architects	by detectives
to surround	to paint
with chopsticks	to write
Mercedes cars	to assassinate
by Christopher Columbus	War and Peace
from Colombia	to rule
	Guernica

Hand of death

-ed and -ing adjectives

A   ANALYSIS

1 Look at the film poster.
Which two words describe how the critics felt about the film?
Which two words describe the film?

2 Here are some reactions from people who have just seen *Hand of Death*. Are they talking about their own feelings or describing the film? Tick the correct box.

		own feelings	describing film
a	...boring...	[ ]	[ ]
b	...thrilling...	[ ]	[ ]
c	...horrified...	[ ]	[ ]
d	...petrified...	[ ]	[ ]
e	...disgusting...	[ ]	[ ]
f	...shocked...	[ ]	[ ]

3 Here are some more comments from people who have just seen the film. Are they talking about actors in the film or about the friends they saw the film with? Tick the correct box.

		actor	friend
a	He was really terrifying.	[ ]	[ ]
b	She was totally bored.	[ ]	[ ]
c	He was absolutely disgusting.	[ ]	[ ]
d	She was electrifying.	[ ]	[ ]

Now, can you make any general rules about the use of adjectives ending in *-ed* and *-ing*?

B PRACTICE

4 Each sentence contains one mistake. Find the mistake and correct it.

a Edwin is a charming host; he makes all his guests feel relaxing.

b I thought that meal was disgusted – it tasted revolting!

c Small children can be very infuriating; they often make me feel annoying.

d I am usually confused by cricket; it is certainly complicating!

e Don't expect to be exciting by that play; I thought it was very disappointing.

5 Complete each sentence with either an *-ed* or *-ing* ending to the adjective given.

a Sylvia's skirt split when she ran for the bus, she was very embarrass_____ .

b Ben thinks that book is interest_____ but I was bor_____ when I read it.

c Prices reduced by 50% what an amaz_____ offer!

d I never read the papers. The news usually makes me depress_____.

e English can be very confus_____ for foreigners.

f Looking after children can be exhaust_____. By the end of each day I am usually very tir_____ .

g New York is an excit_____ city and the people are fascinat_____.

h Jane found the rollercoaster an exhilarat_____ experience but I was terrif_____ by it!

C COMMUNICATION

6 Work in pairs or small groups. You work for an advertising agency. Your job is to think of slogans for these posters. Make slogans like the example, using the adjectives given.

worried ... relaxed

boring ... exciting

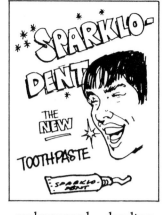

boring ... amazed   embarrassed ... dazzling

Now, as a group, write a short slogan for a radio commercial for new 'Clean-o-eeze' washing powder. Try to use *-ed* and *-ing* adjectives in your slogan.

D TEST

7 Complete each gap with the correct word from this list.

> charming bored relaxing disgusting
> tired appalling invigorating
> interested exciting fascinating

Bath is a small city about 150 kilometres west of London. It was founded in the first century by the Romans who had discovered the (**a**) _____ hot springs. It is easy to imagine the Roman soldiers, (**b**) _____ and exhausted from a busy day fighting the natives, (**c**) _____ in their luxurious hot swimming pools! After the Roman era the city declined in importance but it was rediscovered by the upper classes in the eighteenth century. Wealthy aristocrats, (**d**) _____ with life on their country estates, came to Bath to enjoy the (**e**) _____ social scene and to 'take the waters'. In fact the local mineral water tastes quite (**f**) _____, but people believed it had medicinal qualities and could cure some of the (**g**) _____ diseases which were common at the time. Fortunately, today's visitors are more (**h**) _____ in the (**i**) _____ architecture and (**j**) _____ history than in the rather unpleasant water!

Describing objects

Order of adjectives before a noun

A ANALYSIS

1 Read through these remarks made by people and match them with the pictures above.

a 'They've moved into a delightful, tiny, wooden chalet. You must go and see it!'

b 'She's just bought a set of three amazing nineteenth-century Russian pearl rings.'

c 'Have you seen his new car? It's an extremely expensive, two-year-old, bright red Italian sports car.'

d 'John has just put a deposit on a little modern brick-built terraced house.'

e 'He's given her his grandmother's beautiful, antique, gold wedding ring.'

f 'I really don't like the car that she bought for me. It's the most disgusting, old, brown heap you can imagine.'

2 Answer these questions about the sentences in exercise 1.

a Sentences a, b, e and f all contain adjectives expressing opinion. Which ones are they?

a .....   e .....

b .....   f .....

b Which sentence contains a number which qualifies the noun? Where does the number come, before or after the adjectives?

c Three sentences contain an adjective which is often used to describe the noun, and which changes the meaning slightly, called a defining adjective. Although used as an adjective, this can sometimes be a noun, for example, *wine glass*. Which sentences use words like this? _____,

_____, _____.

Which words are used in these sentences to define the noun?

_____, _____, _____.

d Most of the adjectives in the sentences above fall into the categories below. Write the adjectives in the correct categories:

Age: _____

Colour: _____

Defining adjective/noun: _____

Material: _____

Nationality: _____

Opinion: _____

Size: _____

One is left, which one? _____

For the purposes of this exercise, we'll call this general.

3 Now use the sentences in exercise 1 to decide if the following sentences about the order of the adjectives are true (T) or false (F). Correct the false ones.

	TRUE	FALSE
a Number comes first.	[ ]	[ ]
b Colour comes before age.	[ ]	[ ]
c Defining adjectives/nouns (see 2c) come directly before the noun.	[ ]	[ ]
d Size comes before age.	[ ]	[ ]
e Material comes before nationality.	[ ]	[ ]
f Nationality comes before colour.	[ ]	[ ]
g Opinion comes after size.]	[ ]	[ ]

Can you now complete this chart showing the order?

number _____ ***general*** _____ _____

colour _____ _____ _____ ***noun***

B PRACTICE

4 Put the adjectives in brackets in the correct places in the descriptions below.

a They've just bought two lovely, comfortable, leather chairs.   (black)

_____

b He's got the most incredible, up-to-date computer. (Japanese)

_____

c Our company has just moved into a really elegant white-and-grey office.   (huge)

_____

d I gave them a wedding present of six lovely crystal glasses.   (wine)

_____

e They introduced him to a very tall, red-headed woman.   (beautiful)

_____

f I've just joined a very nice English class.   (small)

_____

g He brought her back very expensive Italian silk shirts.   (several)

_____

h I've just found a pair of silver earrings.   (antique)

_____

5 Put the jumbled adjectives in the right order.

a a car: old/cheap/Polish

_____

b a hi-fi system: modern/black/attractive/plastic

_____

c a table: dining/smoked glass/modern/Swedish

_____

d a policeman: tall/good-looking/Scottish

_____

e a hat: hard/fibre-glass/riding/black

_____

f a pencil: lead/yellow/short

_____

g a lamp: table/burgundy/ceramic

_____

h a poodle: French/brown-and-white/small

_____
_____

C COMMUNICATION

6 Think of two or three adjectives to describe each of the pictures above. Then write a sentence to describe the picture, using your adjectives.

Work in pairs: read your sentences out to your partner. Now combine all the adjectives the two of you have used to make one long sentence.

Compare your sentences with other groups around the class.

D TEST

7 Choose from the adjectives below to complete the sentences.

> American expensive French grey huge interesting long leather Persian red science-fiction six-week-old tiny three twenty-first century

a I've just read a really _____, _____ book about a _____, _____, _____ space station.

b Have you seen my cat? It's a _____, _____ , _____, _____ kitten.

c You can't miss her. She's wearing a _____, _____, _____ coat.

d She gave me _____, _____, _____ perfumes for Christmas.

References

Position of adverbs

A ANALYSIS

1 Patricia Kendall is the Managing Director of Kendall Designs Ltd. She is looking for a new administrative manager and has shortlisted two applicants. Here are the references from their present employers:

a Who do you think is best for the job?

b Circle all the adverbs in the two references. (Three have already been done for you.)

THE HENDERSON CORPORATION
Henderson House
Leaborough Trading Estate
Leaborough LE9 9OX

CONFIDENTIAL REFERENCE: JOANNA GOLDSMITH

Joanna Goldsmith is (currently) employed as our deputy admin manager. She has already been promoted twice within this company. She is never sick although she sometimes arrives late in the mornings. She performs well in all her tasks and hardly ever makes mistakes. Joanna also has a very friendly personality. I occasionally feel that her talents are wasted in an administrative job. However, I can definitely recommend her for the position you are offering.

Sincerely

M. R. McWhite

M R. McWhite
Personnel Manager

HICKTON BENNET & CO *SOLICITORS*
23 High Street
Brackton
Middlesex

Private and Confidential

Dear Ms Kendall

Re: Reference for Stephen Briggs

Stephen has worked as my assistant since 1989. He is intelligent and dedicated and has always been punctual; in fact he is (usually) the first person to arrive in the mornings. He really enjoys administrative work and often does extra work at home in the evenings.

However, I have noticed that he works badly when under pressure and rarely socialises with his colleagues. He doesn't (really) get involved with people at work.

Yours sincerely

Christina Bolton

Christina Bolton
Administrative Officer

2 Answer these questions and give an example sentence from the letters in exercise 1.

a Where do most adverbs go in sentences?
Example: _____

b What happens when there is more than one part to the verb, for example *has been promoted* or *doesn't get involved*?
Example: _____

c What happens when there is a modal verb, for example *can recommend*?
Example: _____

d What happens when the verb is *am, are, is or were*?
Example: _____

e Which two adverbs always go after the main verb?
Example: _____

B PRACTICE

3 Re-write these sentences to include the adverb in brackets.

a She's been to New York.   (never)

_____

b I can answer that question.   (easily)

_____

c He is late because of the traffic.   (occasionally)

_____

d I eat when I go to my mother's house.   (well)

_____

e Percy doesn't like spicy food.   (really)

_____

f Tourists should carry their passports with them.   (always)

_____

g I have started learning Arabic.   (recently)

_____

h Children behave when they are tired.   (badly)

_____

_____

4 Complete these sentences by putting the words in brackets into the correct order.

a Amsterdam _____ as the Venice of the North.
(usually/known/is)

b My parents _____ abroad in their lives.
(never/been/have)

c You _____ such foolish advice.
(taken/have/should/never)

d I _____ after a hard day's work.
(sleep/always/well)

e That poor child _____ a proper meal.
(hardly ever/has/eaten)

C GAME

5 Who am I?
Imagine you are a famous person. Write five sentences about yourself. Each sentence must contain an adverb. Look at this example:
　　I often visit foreign countries.
　　I have never done any cooking or cleaning.
　　I really love dogs and horses.
　　I usually live in a very large house in London.
　　I am always treated with a lot of respect.

Take it in turns to read your sentences to the other students. The student who correctly guesses who you are gets one point. The winner of the game is the student who has the most points at the end.

D TEST

6 Some of these sentences are incorrect. Find the mistakes and write out the corrected version if necessary.

a I usually badly sleep when I am worried about something.

_____

b You must really learn to listen to your teacher.

_____

c Henry's team easily has beaten all the others.

_____

d Sophia rarely is late for her lessons.

_____

e Is Emma coming definitely to the theatre with us?

_____

f My family has lived always on a farm.

_____

g Soldiers obey usually their officers.

_____

h I don't work well when I'm under pressure.

_____

i Children should listen always to their parents.

_____

j In historic times most people frequently were ill.

_____

All in the home

Prepositions of location

A ANALYSIS

1 Look at the picture and write the correct numbers after each sentence.

a The woman is *at* the door.   *3*
b The child is _____ the sink.   _____
c The dog is _____ the child.   _____
d The cat is _____ the fridge.   _____
e The plates are _____ the sink.   _____
f The saucepans are _____ the cooker.   _____
g The chair is _____ the cooker.   _____
h The tea-towel is _____ the cooker.   _____
i The food is _____ the fridge.   _____
j The woman is _____ the child.   _____

2 Now write these prepositions in the correct gaps above.

at	behind	by	in	in front of
near	next to	on	under	opposite

B PRACTICE

3 Complete the gaps with a suitable preposition.

a I'll wait for you _____ the bus stop.
b He's got the secret documents _____ his case.
c Make sure that you sit _____ me at the concert so that we can talk to each other.
d Put the plates _____ the table, will you, then we can eat?
e This flat has so little storage room that I have to keep my suitcases _____ the bed.
f Do you know Geraldine? Yes, she lives _____ me; just on the other side of the road.
g Don't turn round! There's something horrible _____ you!
h Leave the parcel _____ the door; I'll pick it up.

4 Read the leaflet below about safety in the home and complete the advice with prepositions. Can you think of any other pieces of advice? Tell your partner if you can.

SAFETY IN THE HOME

TIPS You should always make sure that your home is safe. Follow these simple guidelines:

DO
- put a guard _____ an open fire
- keep tools and other sharp objects _____ a cupboard
- keep medicines _____ closed doors
- encourage your children to keep their toys _____ a toy box
- keep a fire extinguisher _____ the cooker

DON'T
- put vases of flowers _____ the television
- hang clothes _____ a fire or an electric heater
- run electrical wires _____ a carpet
- stand _____ chairs or stools
- leave sharp knives _____ the work surfaces in the kitchen

C COMMUNICATION

5 Work in pairs.

Student A: Look at the picture on the bottom left of the page.
Student B: Look at the picture on the bottom right of the page.
You each have a picture of a room. In that room there are nine hidden objects. Find the objects and describe their position to your partner. Can you find any differences? What is the profession of the owner of the room?

D TEST

6 Re-write these sentences in the correct order, making sure that you use the prepositions correctly.

a Where shall I put this vase?
it/table/in/lounge/the/the/put/on

b Let me take your photo here;
and/lovely/in front of/behind/stand/the/that/fountain/bush

c Where shall I wait for you?
wait/by/bench/the/on/the/river

d Can these animals be put together?
can/cat/dog/fish/put/the/you/the/the/but/near/not/next to

e Where is the complaints desk?
the/at/main/under/it's/the/stairs/entrance

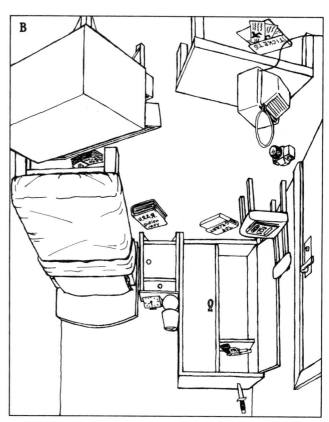

Michael Jackson

Prepositions of time

A ANALYSIS

1 Read this text about Michael Jackson and complete the details in the chart on the right.

Michael Jackson was born on 29 August 1958. By the age of five he was singing with his brothers in The Jackson Five. He turned professional at nine and he's been appearing in the charts regularly since the age of eleven, when The Jackson Five went on their first tour. From the age of five till the late 1970s he continued singing with his brothers, but during that time it became clear that Michael had a career of his own to follow. Since 1978 he has been a solo performer, and for the last few years he has been producing mega hits like *Thriller* and *Bad*. He has also been pursuing a film career, with his first appearance in *Oz*, as the scarecrow, in 1975, and, more recently, *Moonwalker*. He is often in the studio during the week, at church on Sundays (he's a dedicated Jehovah's Witness) and relaxing at home with his pet chimpanzee at the weekend.

MICHAEL JACKSON	
Born	_____
Turned professional	_____
First tour	_____
First chart single	_____
First film appearance	_____
Went solo	_____
Likes	_____

2 Read the passage again and underline all the prepositions connected with time.

3 Now find the prepositions below in the passage and decide what follows them (e.g. an age, a date etc.). Complete as much of the chart as you can with ticks, like the example.

Can you add more ticks to the chart? Use the phrases below to help you:

| at six o'clock | by two thirty | during 1989 |
| in spring | during the summer | at Easter |

	age	day	date	year	period of time	time	season	festival
at	✓							
by	✓							
during								
for								
from ... till	✓							
in								
on								
since	✓							

4 Which prepositions are usually used to express:
a point in time (time, day, date etc.)
a period of time/duration

B PRACTICE

5 Put prepositions in the gaps.

a _____ Monday **b** _____ 1956
c _____ 24 March **d** _____ winter
e _____ the age of 12 **f** _____ Christmas
g _____ half past six **h** _____ the lunch hour
i _____ the weekend **j** _____ the evening
k _____ 11.00 a.m. **l** _____ 3.00 p.m.
m _____ two hours **n** _____ night

6 Write these telexes out in full, making sure that you use the correct prepositions.

```
1  FREE CHRISTMAS. WOULD LIKE TO VISIT. CAN COME 24TH, 18.00.
   STAY 29TH. PERHAPS COULD VISIT GRAN DURING PERIOD. PHONE
   ME SUNDAY 10.00 - 11.30.
```

```
2  ELENA LOPEZ BORN 1973. NOW AGE 18. THOUGHT TO BE IN
   COLOMBIA 1987/89. RIOTS OF 1989 IN CHINA. FIND HER.
```

```
3  LUCY ARRIVED LONDON MAY. WITH ME JUNE - NOV. WANTS TO GO
   TO SWITZERLAND WINTER. WOULD LIKE TO STAY WITH YOU 3
   MONTHS NOV - FEB. I NEED TO KNOW OCTOBER.
```

C COMMUNICATION

7 Work in pairs. Write a few notes about your own life, or a friend's, or a famous person's. Try to include information as in the paragraph about Michael Jackson. Then tell your partner about you/your friend, and he/she makes a biodata form.

D TEST

8 Look at the following biodata and then complete the paragraph below.

```
MAXINE DWYER
Born   11 May 1963
First stage appearance   winter season/Christmas 1979
Film career   bit parts 1980 – 84
First starring role   1985
Leading lady in romantic films   1986 – present
Likes  weekdays – working hard
       Saturday – walking the dogs
       Sunday   – playing sport
```

Maxine Dwyer was born (**a**) _____ 1963, (**b**) _____ 11 May. Her first stage appearance was in pantomime, (**c**) _____ Christmas, (**d**) _____ the winter of 1979. She then had bit parts in a number of films (**e**) _____ 1980/1984. Her first starring role was (**f**) _____ 1985 and she has been a leading lady in romantic films (**g**) _____ 1986. She has a very active home life but (**h**) _____ the week she works very hard, then (**i**) _____ weekends she plays hard, often spending all day Saturday walking her dogs and playing sport (**j**) _____ Sundays.

An eventful day!

Prepositions and adverbs of time

A ANALYSIS

Dear Graham,

I'm really sorry about lunch earlier today, but let me explain. I went shopping at about nine this morning and just after I left the supermarket I had a car crash. Nothing serious, and my local garage said they could fix it while I was out during the day. I was due at the dentist's at ten, but I was half an hour late and then I had to wait for another half an hour before he could see me. I finally left at about quarter to twelve, and just as I was leaving I met Angela, who kept me talking for ages!

Anyway, I eventually got to the travel agent's at one to find they were closed until two, so I went to the bank and got my travellers' cheques. I got back to the travel agent's at two but they were late back and then I had to wait until they'd found the right tickets! And they weren't even apologetic that I'd been waiting since two! I ran to the restaurant, hoping to get there before about 2.30, but when I arrived at the restaurant you'd gone (not surprisingly). I tried to ring you to tell you about all the awful things that had happened since I left you last night, but I had no luck, and, anyway, I had to collect the car at 3.30 and get home - if I'd arrived after four I'd have missed the taxi to the airport. Well, that's it. I'll have to go now - they're calling my flight. Sorry again and I'll see you next week.

Love, Maria

2 Go through the text again and underline all the occurrences of these words: *after, as, before, during, for, since, until, when, while.*
Now write the words which follow them:

after	I left the supermarket I had a crash	for	_____
as	_____	since	_____
before	_____	until	_____
during	_____	when	_____
		while	_____

1 Here are the events from Maria's day. Put them into the correct order. Then write approximate times next to them.

		order	time
a	She went to the travel agent's.	[ ]	___
b	She went to the restaurant.	[ ]	___
c	She took the car to the garage.	[ ]	___
d	She went to the airport.	[ ]	___
e	She met Angela.	[ ]	___
f	She went to the supermarket.	[1]	9.00
g	She went back to the travel agent's.	[ ]	___
h	She collected the car from the garage.	[ ]	___
i	She went to the bank.	[ ]	___
j	She saw the dentist.	[ ]	___
k	She went to the dentist's.	[ ]	___
l	She had a car crash.	[ ]	___

3 Using the information in exercise 2, complete this chart.

	can be followed by	
	a clause	**a noun**
after		
as		
before		
during		
for		
since		
until		
when		
while		

B PRACTICE

4 Match the two halves of each sentence to make as many sentences as you can.

a The bus arrived
b The two girls were singing
c I got to the party
d You really don't have time to shop
e We really must visit the sights
f He hasn't done anything like that
g I've been waiting here
h The room fell silent
i You mustn't make a decision
j She'll let you know the answer

1 when most of the guests had left.
2 as I walked in.
3 before the end of the holiday.
4 after I had been waiting for an hour.
5 for over two hours.
6 when she's made a decision.
7 while they were working.
8 until you're sure it's the right one.
9 during the lunch hour.
10 since I've known him.

5 Choose the best alternatives for the gaps.

a Why don't you make a cup of coffee (during/while/until) _____ I'm finishing this?
b He's already waited (until/since/for) _____ six weeks to find out.
c Can I read the book (while/before/when) _____ you've finished it?
d You must have seen this sofa. I've had it (since/for/after) _____ I moved here last year.
e Don't interrupt her (while/for/during) _____ her lesson.
f I knew him (before/since/while) _____ I came here.

C COMMUNICATION

6 Work in pairs.

Student A: Look at the pictures at the top of the page.
Student B: Look at the pictures at the bottom of the page.

Make notes about each picture, then describe them to your partner, using the words and expressions from exercise 2. Together, all the pictures make a story. Put them in the right order with your partner and retell the story.

D TEST

7 Fill in the gaps with a suitable preposition or adverb of time.

a Can you wait till the afternoon? I'll come _____ lunch.
b She's been living in this house _____ her husband died.
c I bought the perfume _____ I was living in France.
d He got that wound _____ the war.
e They were in the restaurant _____ more than four hours.
f Will you do the tidying-up _____ your parents arrive? I'd like the place to look nice.
g I'd like you to meet my friends. Can you stay here _____ they arrive?
h He didn't see the end of the film. He didn't wait _____ the end.
i I only saw Len briefly. He arrived just _____ I was leaving.
j Please don't talk to me _____ I'm on the phone!

Can you count it?

Countable and uncountable nouns

A ANALYSIS

ACME Accommodation Agency

for flats and houses

tel: 777 0099

Eastern Philosophy Centre

HEALTH HAPPINESS CONTENTMENT

tel: 909 3030

Chandler Detective Agency

RESEARCH ADVICE INVESTIGATIONS

Tel: 016 7890

GRAND FURNITURE SALE

a few chairs & tables, a lot of sofas & armchairs still unsold
JENKINS DISCOUNT WAREHOUSE

SMITHSON Social Club

HOBBIES TRAVEL
MUSIC EXCITEMENT
PARTIES FUN

Want to find out more about us?
Tel: 066 7986

VISIT THE LAKE DISTRICT
Stay at one of our many charming hotels or guest houses . . .
but don't forget your walking boots because there's so much
beautiful countryside to explore and a lot of spectacular
scenery is just waiting to be discovered . . . and it's all free!
For more information call 0800 990 1122

1 English nouns are either countable or uncountable. Look at the advertisements and put all the circled nouns into one of these categories. The first four have been done for you.

countable	uncountable
agency	accommodation
flats	furniture
_____	_____
_____	_____
_____	_____
_____	_____
_____	_____
_____	_____
_____	_____
_____	_____

2 What are the differences between the two types of noun? Study the use of the nouns in the advertisements and complete this summary.

		countable	uncountable
	a/an	[ ]	[ ]
They can	the	[ ]	[ ]
be used	much	[ ]	[ ]
with these	many	[ ]	[ ]
words:	a lot of	[ ]	[ ]
	a few	[ ]	[ ]
They have a plural form.		[ ]	[ ]
They take a singular verb.		[ ]	[ ]

B PRACTICE

3 Complete this dialogue by choosing the correct form of the words in brackets.

A Excuse me, is this the (**a**) (information/ informations) desk?

B Yes, madam, how can I help you?

A Well, you see I have a lot of (**b**) (luggage/luggages), and I want some (**c**) (advice/advices) about taking it on the plane to Paris.

B (**d**) (Does/Do) your (**e**) (baggage/baggages) weigh more than twenty kilos?

A I'm not sure, you see I have (**f**) (many/a lot of) photographic (**g**) (ment/equipments), (**h**) (It's/ They're) all rather heavy.

B I'm afraid twenty kilos is the maximum allowance for a (**i**) (travel/journey) within Europe. If you want to take more than that you'll need special (**j**) (permission/permissions) from the airline.

4 Each of these sentences contains one or two mistakes. Find the mistakes and then re-write the sentences correctly.

a My sister is very clever – she knows so much facts.

_____

b I'm doing a research into Chinese history for my degree.

_____

c Antique English furnitures are very expensive.

_____

d I like two spoonfuls of sugars with my coffee.

_____

e Mathematics are difficult for me.

_____

f My father gives me too many advices.

_____

g Travel? I hate them.

_____

h English has too much words and too many grammar!

_____

C COMMUNICATION

5 Work with a partner. Student A has some famous sayings and quotations, but each one has a missing uncountable noun. The first letter of each missing word has been given to help you. Student B has a clue for each missing word. How fast can you work out the missing words and complete the phrases?

Student A:
SAYINGS

a You can't buy h_____.

b There is no p_____ for the wicked.

c T_____ broadens the mind.

d A little k_____ is a dangerous thing.

QUOTATIONS

e A _____ is seldom welcome, and those who need it the most always like it the least.

f Architecture is frozen m_____.

g I love w_____. I can sit and look at it for hours.

h P_____ is the politeness of kings.

Student B:
CLUES

a feeling good **b** opposite of war **c** take a journey
d opposite of ignorance **e** you give this if someone has a problem **f** Mozart and Beethoven wrote a lot of this. **g** doing a job **h** don't be late

Do you know who said these things?

D TEST

6 Choose the correct word to fill the gap in each sentence.

a I hate reading newspapers, the news (is/are) _____ always so depressing.

b So many beautiful views, such wonderful (scenery/ sceneries) _____.

c The witness gave (much/many) _____ useful evidence to the police.

d Technological progress (was/were) _____ very rapid in the 1960s.

e Our teacher gave us (a lot of/a few) _____ help with our project.

f We have lots of (homework/homeworks) _____ every week.

g The Lake District has so (many/much) _____ lovely countryside.

h We are conducting (a/some) _____ research into smoking habits.

i I don't drink (much/many) _____ coffee these days.

j Happiness (is/are) _____ more important than dollars.

This is the life!

The use of the definite article

A ANALYSIS

1 Are these statements about the letter true (T) or false (F)?

a Jeanette doesn't like village life. [ ]
b She is more afraid in the country than in the city. [ ]
c She lives in the main street of the village. [ ]
d She's probably a doctor or a nurse. [ ]
e Her son, Sam, doesn't like school any more. [ ]
f Her friend Mary also works in the hospital. [ ]

2 The following phrases all come from the letter. Each of them contains a noun (in italics). Look at the letter again and decide whether the noun is a general one, or if it is specific.

	specific	general
a *life* in the country seems better ...		
b the *life* I lived in London ...		
c we learn to live with *fear* ...		
d the *fear* of wasps and bees ...		
e the *village* is lovely ...		
f the *garden* is delightful ...		
g the *street* I live in ...		
h I'm used to the *hospital* ...		
i Dad's been in *hospital* ...		
j Sam's happy with the *school* here.		
k You'd love the *shop* where Mary works ...		
l he doesn't hate *school* any more ...		

Dear Stephen

Well, I'm certainly settling down here in my new home. Welton is a lovely village, and already life in the country seems better than in the city: more relaxed, safer. The life I lived in London was so stressful in comparison. I know we learn to live with fear in the city with all the accidents, burglaries and so on, but here all I've got is the fear of wasps and bees! The village is lovely; so is my cottage, and the garden is delightful. The street I live in has lots of pretty cottages with colourful gardens, and no traffic! I'm getting used to the hospital too — oh, I didn't tell you, did I - Dad's been in hospital recently, nothing serious, he broke his wrist. Sam's quite happy with the school here too; he's making lots of friends. I'm lucky, of course, as one of my oldest friends lives here. You'd love the shop where Mary works: it's full of really beautiful ceramics. I'd better go now, Sam is due home any minute, though now that he doesn't hate school any more he's hardly ever in on time!

All the best

Jeanette.

What's the difference between *fear* and *the fear*?
And between *the hospital, the school* and *hospital, school* in this letter?

3 The definite article is always used in English to show that something has been defined, or made specific. There are a number of ways in which we can define things. Look again at these phrases from the letter and decide how each noun is defined.

	relative clause	following phrase	only one	previous mention
the life I lived in London				
the fear of wasps and bees				
the village is lovely				
the garden is delightful				
the street I live in				
I'm used to the hospital				
Sam's happy with the school				
the shop where Mary works				

B PRACTICE

4 Decide whether each of these nouns needs an article.

a Do you like _____ coffee?
b Do you like _____ coffee in that restaurant?
c Don't lean on _____ table; it's not very safe.
d I only have to go to _____ college four days a week.
e _____ church in this village is a very pretty one.
f It's a good exercise. In fact, _____ exercise is essential for your health.
g It's difficult to live without _____ hope.
h That's _____ dog that bit me last week.

5 Find the mistakes in these sentences and correct them.

a Man should try to live with the nature.
b I want to go to the university after leaving the school.
c Where's Sam? I think he's in garden.
d Sun goes round earth.
e I prefer living in city to living in country.
f Town where my brother lives is rather industrial.
g The beauty is in the eye of the beholder.
h The use of the colour makes that painting.

C COMMUNICATION

6 Team game.
Divide into two teams, A and B.
Team A: use Box A below.
Team B: use Box B below.
When your teacher tells you to choose a word from your box, choose one, tell everyone what it is, then write a sentence using it WITHOUT the article. When the other team chooses a word, write a sentence using the word WITH the article. Your teacher will do the scoring.

Box A

hope	science
love	colour
beauty	touch

Box B

hate	sight
art	necessity
anger	fruit

D TEST

7 Fill in the gaps with an article if necessary.

I once taught in a very strange school – an open-air school in Africa. (a) _____ school was really nice, at least when (b) _____ sun was shining! We used to start (c) _____ school at seven in (d) _____ morning but we were usually at (e) _____ home by (f) _____ lunchtime, because of (g) _____ heat. Some of our better students went on to (h) _____ college, which was a great source of (i) _____ pride to them and their parents, as (j) _____ education was considered a great privilege in those days and was not available to everyone.

A night at the movies

Question tags

A   ANALYSIS

1 Read the conversation and decide whether the
statements below are true (T) or false (F).

Chuck	Well, what did you think of it?
Sue	Not bad, but the plot was rather obvious, wasn't it?
Chuck	I didn't think so. Anyway, I loved the special effects.
Sue	But that explosion didn't look very realistic, did it?
Chuck	No, you could see it was a model, couldn't you?
Sue	Yes, still, the acting was pretty good.
Chuck	Well, that's a matter of opinion. The hero wasn't very convincing, was he?
Sue	He was certainly very handsome!
Chuck	We've seen him on TV, haven't we?
Sue	Mm, I think so. Now, let's get something to eat, shall we?
Chuck	Okay, so long as we don't talk about that film any more!

	TRUE	FALSE
a Sue expects Chuck to agree that the plot was obvious.		
b Chuck thinks that the explosion looked realistic.		
c Chuck expects Sue to agree that the hero wasn't convincing.		
d Sue thinks that Chuck will probably want to eat something.		

2 To make a question tag, we have to look at the
subject and the verb or auxiliary verb in the first part
of the sentence.

Example:

The plot was rather obvious, wasn't it.
The plot ———————————————► it.
      was ———————► wasn't

We've seen him on TV, haven't we?
We ———————————————► we
(have) seen ——————► haven't

Now complete this chart by looking at the examples
in the dialogue.

sentence verb	question tag	sentence subject	question tag
was	——► wasn't	the plot	——► it
didn't look	——►	the hero	——►
could see	——►	you	——►
have seen	——►	we	——►

What did you notice about the question tag for 'Let's ...'?

B PRACTICE

3 Match each sentence with its correct question tag.

a	He was a brilliant actor,	**1**	had she?
b	The heroine's American,	**2**	would they?
c	Children wouldn't like it,	**3**	couldn't he?
d	Let's buy some popcorn,	**4**	hasn't he?
e	John's been to Hollywood,	**5**	don't they?
f	Maria hasn't seen that film,	**6**	wasn't he?
g	They make worse films nowadays,	**7**	will they?
		8	shall we?
h	Your parents won't go to the cinema,	**9**	isn't she?
i	She hadn't seen it before,	**10**	has she?
j	Hitchcock could really make good films,		

4 When Sue and Chuck got to the restaurant they continued their discussion of the film. Complete the missing question tags from their conversation.

Chuck Some of the songs were rather ridiculous, (**a**) _____?

Sue Yes, and that old actress really couldn't sing, (**b**) _____?

Chuck No, you know she hasn't been in a big film for years, (**c**) _____ 11?

Sue No. Still, the locations looked marvellous, (**d**) _____?

Chuck Fabulous! I always love films set in Brazil.

Sue We really should visit South America some day, (**e**) _____?

Chuck Only if you're paying!

Sue That reminds me, let's ask for the bill, (**f**) _____?

5 Fill in the gaps with the correct verb forms.

a The meal _____ very good, was it?

b _____ go out somewhere tonight, shall we?

c Michael _____ dance very well, can't he?

d Hilary _____ from Canada, isn't she?

e Your parents _____ like me, do they?

f Yuri _____ see a doctor, shouldn't he?

C GAME

TONIGHT'S GAME:
"Don't say Yes or No"

That's right ✓   Yes! ✗
You're quite correct! ✓
That's not true ✓
No! ✗   That's true ✓
That's not right ✓

How long can you answer questions without saying 'Yes' or 'No'???

6 Don't say yes or no!
Work in large groups. Each person must take it in turn to answer questions asked by the group. You are not allowed to say 'yes' or 'no' but you must answer every question properly. As soon as you say 'yes' or 'no' you are out. The person who can last the longest without saying 'yes' or 'no' is the winner. (If you are asking questions, remember that one of the best ways to get someone to say 'yes' or 'no' is to use questions tags!)

D TEST

7 Add a suitable question tag to each of these sentences.

a Mum and dad will be coming later, _____?

b Clint Eastwood is your favourite movie star, _____?

c That old cinema wasn't very comfortable, _____?

d Walt Disney films can be very entertaining, _____?

e Let's see the new James Bond film, _____?

f Jane's never been to a horror film, _____?

g The British don't make many films, _____?

h Your brother hates romantic movies, _____?

i We really shouldn't complain, _____?

j You won't tell the police, _____?

Anyone for tennis?

All, both, every, each, none, neither

A ANALYSIS

COURT 1	COURT 2	COURT 3

1 Look at the picture and decide whether the following sentences are true (T) or false (F).

                                                                letter

a All of the people are playing tennis. [　]

b Both of the boys are wearing white
shorts. [　]   **A,B**

c Both of the girls on court 2 are
wearing skirts. [　]

d Every girl is wearing a skirt. [　]

e None of the girls is wearing glasses. [　]

f Each girl is wearing a black t-shirt. [　]

g Neither of the boys is wearing black
shorts. [　]

h Both of the boys are wearing black
shoes. [　]

i Both of the girls on court 3 are
wearing trousers. [　]

j None of the players is hitting the ball. [　]

k None of the girls is wearing a black
T-shirt. [　]

l All of the girls are sitting down. [　]

2 Go back to exercise 1. Look at the true sentences and in the column headed *letter* write the letters relating to the boys and girls mentioned. For example, for **b** you write **A, B**.

3 Now use the sentences in exercise 1 to complete the chart below. The first row has been done for you.

	verb		focus		number		
	sing.	*plural*	*affirm.*	*neg.*	*sing.*	*dual*	*more than 2*
all both each every neither none		✓	✓				✓

4 Now go back to exercise 1 and correct the sentences that were false.

B PRACTICE

5 Complete the following sentences about the picture.

a _____ people _____ playing badminton.

b _____ the girls _____ long hair.

c _____ the boys _____ hitting the ball.

d _____ player _____ on court.

e _____ girl on court 2 _____ wearing a
white T-shirt.

f _____ girl _____ wearing white trainers,
except for E.

6 Look at the picture below then complete the sentences.

  a Both of the dummies are wearing skirts.
  b All of the T-shirts _____
  c None of the dummies _____
  d Neither of the skirts _____
  e Each pair of shorts _____
  f Both short-sleeved blouses _____
  g Every long-sleeved blouse _____
  h Both pairs of shorts _____

C COMMUNICATION

7 Work with the picture above. Give the clothes prices, colours (using whatever pens and pencils you have available) and patterns (e.g. stripes, flowers, check, dots etc.). When you have finished, describe your picture to your partner, using *both, all, each, every,* *none* and *neither.* Your partner makes a copy of what you have drawn. Then ask your partner questions about his/her picture and follow the instructions you are given. When you have finished, compare the pictures.

D TEST

8 Choose the correct forms to complete the sentences.

  a (Both/Neither/Each) _____ of my brothers have dark hair.
  b (None/Every/All) _____ of the people here knows how to speak English.
  c (All/Both/Every) _____ person has the right to vote.
  d (Both/None/Neither) _____ game is too easy for me.
  e I have lots of friends and (both/all/each) _____ of them live near me.

  f (Every/Both/Each) _____ of these is nice. I don't know which to choose.
  g (Each/All/Both) _____ of the sexes have their good and bad points.
  h Daddy, have we seen (both/every/all) _____ of the animals now? No, but we've seen most of them.
  i Which of these two restaurants do you want to go to? (Every/Neither/All) _____ of them.
  j I've lived here for over five years and I've seen (every/both/none) _____ of the sights!

My secret desire

Wish + would or wish + past simple?

A   ANALYSIS

1   Look at the picture. What is everybody thinking?
Complete the sentences.

Carla   I wish _____ was _____ rock star.
Jim   I wish _____ would _____ me.
Maria   I wish my teacher _____ give me
_____ _____ _____.
Tom   I wish _____ _____ a millionaire.
Teacher   I wish _____ _____ on holiday.

2   We can divide these wishes into two types. The first
type of wish shows regret about a situation and a
wish that it was different. The second type of wish
shows a desire for an action to take place – for
somebody else to do something.

Write down two examples of each type from the
sentences above and complete the grammar
summary below.

Regret about a situation
_____
_____
_____
I wish + subject + _____

Desire for an action by someone else
_____
_____
_____
I wish + subject + _____ + _____

B PRACTICE

3 Choose the correct word/s to fill the gaps.

a Stavros is overweight, I wish he _____ on a diet.
(i) would go   (ii) went

b I hate my hair, I wish I _____ curly hair.
(i) would have   (ii) had

c My salary is very low, I wish I _____ more.
(i) would earn   (ii) earned

d I smoke too much, I wish I _____ such a heavy smoker.
(i) wouldn't be   (ii) wasn't

e I'm fed up with that car, I wish somebody _____ it.
(i) would steal   (ii) stole

f Now that I'm 60 I sometimes wish I _____ younger.
(i) would be   (ii) was

g I often wish English grammar _____ easier.
(i) would be   (ii) was

h Jenny wears awful clothes, I wish she _____ something nicer.
(i) would buy   (ii) bought

4 What would you say in these situations? Write sentences beginning *I wish ...*
Examples
You think you are too short.
I wish I was taller.
You think John should get his hair cut.
I wish John would get his hair cut.

a You think the government should reduce taxes.

_____

b You are a student but you would rather be a teacher.

_____

c You are a secretary but you would like to be a film director.

_____

d You believe that rich countries ought to help poor ones.

_____

e You want to learn to drive. Your uncle is a driving instructor.

_____

f Your English isn't as good as you would like it to be.

_____

C GAME

MY SECRET DESIRE
the game that exposes people's innermost desires!
But can you guess whose desires they are???

5 Take a piece of paper and fold it in half. On one side write three sentences:

a What you would secretly like to be.
b Something about yourself that you secretly wish was different.
c Something you would like somebody else to do.

Then write 'Who am I?' underneath your sentences. Look at the example:

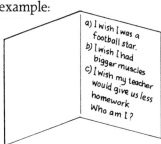

a) I wish I was a football star.
b) I wish I had bigger muscles
c) I wish my teacher would give us less homework
Who am I?

Then fold your paper in half and hand it to the teacher. The papers will be mixed up and handed out again. When you receive your new piece of paper, try to guess who has written it and write his or her name on the other side, then hand it back to your teacher. Your teacher will then hand each piece of paper to the person whose name is written on the back. Each person must read out the sentences on the paper they have been given and the rest of the class decides whether these are your real secret desires or not.

D TEST

6 Complete the sentences using the verbs in brackets.

a My parents are always criticising my clothes. I wish they (stop) _____ doing it.
b I wish I (be) _____ more musical. I can't play any instruments.
c Your father is so nice. I wish he (be) _____ my father too.
d Women never get treated equally in this country. I wish the government (do) _____ something about it.
e I wish my son (get) _____ a haircut. He looks like a hippy.
f I hate living in the city. I wish I (live) _____ in the country.
g Chemistry lessons are so boring. I wish the teacher (make) _____ them more interesting.
h I'm so lonely. I wish I (have) _____ more friends.
i I can never see anything in a crowd. I wish I (be) _____ taller.
j Hamburgers again! I wish you (cook) _____ something different for a change!

Index of structures (alphabetical)